To

_____

From

_____

Date

_____

STORIES OF *Love* TO WARM THE HEART

True Stories of Hope and Inspiration

EDITED BY JAMES STUART BELL

Guideposts

Stories of Love to Warm the Heart

ISBN-10: 0-8249-4937-4
ISBN-13: 978-0-8249-4937-2

Published by Guideposts
16 East 34th Street
New York, New York 10016
Guideposts.org

Distributed by Ideals Publications, a Guideposts company
2630 Elm Hill Pike, Suite 100
Nashville, Tennessee 37214

Guideposts and *Ideals* are registered trademarks of Guideposts.

Cover and interior design by Thinkpen Design, Inc., www.thinkpendesign.com
Cover art/photo by Shutterstock
Typeset by Thinkpen Design, Inc.

Printed and bound in China
10 9 8 7 6 5 4 3 2 1

Contents

Introduction

First Corinthians 13 paints a beautiful portrait of love: "Love is patient, love is kind. It does not envy, it does not boast, it is not proud. It does not dishonor others, it is not self-seeking, it is not easily angered, it keeps no record of wrongs. Love does not delight in evil but rejoices with the truth. It always protects, always trusts, always hopes, always perseveres. Love never fails."

In this heartwarming collection, enjoy reading about the myriad ways we give and receive love: between God and us, husband and wife, friend to friend. They'll remind you of the many forms of love—for it's love which makes it possible for us to practice patience, kindness, humbleness, forgiveness, compassion, hope, perseverance, and trust. And ultimately, these stories will point you back to the One who is love Himself.

We can spend our whole lives diving into this love; understanding it and feeling it more and more until it permeates every aspect of our lives. As Mark Stubbs says in his story about recognizing God's love for the first time, "Not my love, or my wife's love...but a love so all-encompassing it will take a lifetime to grasp. To know that love, to grow in it and serve it—at last I've found the ultimate challenge."

The stories in this joyous volume go way beyond red roses and sunset walks: they're poignant reminders of this best-of-all gift from God: love.

How Love Endures

BY EVELYN HUSBAND

It was a year I could never have imagined happening, let alone getting through. In 2003, I lost the love of my life, the man I expected to be with forever, the man whose face I longed to see when I woke up in the morning. My husband, Rick, was the commander of the space shuttle *Columbia*. On February 1 he was supposed to come home to our two children and me but instead went to his eternal home in heaven when the shuttle broke apart in midair over east Texas.

For some couples, it's love at first sight. For Rick and me, it was love at first date. I had admired Rick from afar since high school in Amarillo, Texas. He was a year older, popular and good-looking. I'd see him singing in choir and starring in school plays, and I couldn't take my eyes off him.

The funny thing is, when we met in college at Texas Tech, Rick was the one staring at me. I was walking to my seat at a basketball game my freshman year and noticed a cute guy with sky-blue eyes watching me. Of course I recognized him. I waved and said hi. Rick was so startled that he didn't say a word...until the next day, when he called and asked me out. (He'd remembered my name and gotten my phone number from the Tech operator.)

Our first date was that Friday, January 28, 1977. Rick stood in my dorm lobby, so tall and handsome. He smiled and I knew it: this guy was special. The evening proved it. There was none of the usual first-date awkwardness—not even when he knocked over his water at dinner and I had to scoot out of the way to avoid getting soaked. We just burst out laughing. I don't remember a thing about the movie we went to except for how right it felt to have his arm around me. Neither of us wanted the night to end. We parked by a lake and looked out at the big Texas sky and talked.

That's when Rick told me about his dream: he wanted to be an astronaut. He'd written to NASA for a list of the requirements: a master's degree in science, math, or Rick's choice, engineering. A daunting number of hours as a fighter pilot—better yet, a test pilot—which was why he was going into the Air Force after graduation. Wow. I was beyond impressed. A man with this kind of passion and commitment was the one I wanted to spend the rest of my life with.

We dated all through college. I loved everything about Rick: his kindness and warmth, his intelligence and integrity and his closeness to his family. I even loved his quirks, like his offbeat sense of humor. His favorite movie was *Young Frankenstein*. The first time I saw it, I could say the lines right along with the actors because I'd heard Rick quote them to me so often. I admired his frugality—Rick would sew up the holes in his socks rather than buy new ones, keep cars until they fell apart (we still have the 1975 Camaro he drove on our first date), and fill up every square millimeter of a note card. I didn't just love Rick, I totally idealized him.

We were married on February 27, 1982, at my church in Amarillo, the same church where my parents and maternal grandparents had their weddings.

I loved being married to Rick. That's not to say we didn't have our rough patches. Rick applied three times to NASA's astronaut program and was rejected. He worked intensely toward his goal, putting in brutal hours in test pilot school at Edwards Air Force Base, then poring over engineering textbooks nights and weekends so he could earn his master's. It meant that we had to spend a lot of time apart. But his dream was my dream, and our time apart ultimately strengthened us for challenges to come.

Right after Rick graduated from test pilot school, I miscarried. Six months later I miscarried again. Each time Rick held me while I wept. "We can't lose our hope, Evey," he said. "God has a plan for us." Our hopes turned into joy in October 1990, when our daughter, Laura, was born. Neither of us could get enough of our sweet girl. Of course, as most couples find, first-time parenthood is equal parts wonder and exhaustion. Often my only respite was reading my Bible while Laura napped. I'd come away energized by God's Word.

I talked to Rick about my growing faith, but he didn't seem to understand. One summer evening in 1991, I found out what was holding him back. Rick told me about some things he had kept bottled up inside for years—mistakes he'd made, doubts and struggles he'd never mentioned for fear of letting people down. We talked all night. Why hadn't Rick shared all of himself with me until now? I wondered. For the first time, I realized he wasn't the flawless being I'd built him up to be.

It was a spiritual wake-up call, as if God were saying, *No one is perfect. Sometimes you will face pressures you can't handle on your own. That's why you need Me.* Ever since we met, I'd put Rick on a pedestal, denied him his human imperfections—a burden he should never have had to bear. *Lord, as much as I love Rick, now more than ever, I know You are the only one who can bear that kind of burden,* I prayed. *Help me learn to put You first in my life.*

Rick was chosen for the US Air Force/British Royal Air Force test pilot exchange program in 1992. That June we moved to the English countryside. Our time abroad gave us an opportunity to focus on building a stronger relationship with God and with each other. Rick searched his heart and discovered something unexpected. "Being an astronaut is not as important as I thought it was," he said one day. "What means the most to me is to try and live my life the way God wants me to...to be a good husband and a good father."

Faith transformed us as a couple. With God at the center of our lives, everything else fell into place. Our marriage grew to a whole deeper level now that no barriers, emotional or spiritual, stood between us. Rick applied a fourth time for the space program and got the call from NASA the same week I found out I was pregnant with our second child.

In Houston, no matter how worn out Rick was after a long day of NASA training, he was 100 percent focused on family at home. Laura would climb on his lap, and he'd read to her. He would pick Matthew up and zoom him through the house like an airplane. There was no sweeter music to me than the sound of our kids laughing with their father.

Maybe that's why I was so anxious at Rick's first shuttle mission, as pilot of the *Discovery* in 1999. The memory of the *Challenger* explosion was also in the back of my mind. I watched *Discovery* lift off from Kennedy Space Center in a plume of smoke and flame. The shuttle climbed in the blue Florida skies. Tears rolled down my cheeks—tears of pride and joy for Rick and our family, and of an overwhelming peace that could come only from God. *Rick's in Your hands now, Lord. You love him even more than I do.*

The *Discovery* mission was a success so I was much more at ease about Rick's next trip, as commander of the shuttle *Columbia*, even though the launch date got pushed back several times to January 16, 2003. We took it in stride. Rick surprised me with a twentieth wedding anniversary trip to San Francisco. We stayed at an English country–style bed-and-breakfast and went for long walks in the hills. What a wonderful reminder of those years in England that had so deepened our commitment—to the Lord and to each other.

Just before he moved into crew quarters for prelaunch quarantine last January, Rick filmed video devotionals for Matthew and Laura. He wanted to surprise each of them with a message from Dad every day that he was in space. My message I discovered on my mirror, in Rick's familiar handwriting with a bar of soap: "I love you, Evey!"

I watched the shuttle lift off last January 16, completely at peace thinking that in a little more than two weeks Rick would be pulling me into his arms and whispering those words in my ear. Then on February 1, as the *Columbia* entered the earth's atmosphere, it broke apart over Texas. It was like watching my whole life break into pieces and fall from the sky.

"Who's going to help me with math?" Laura asked. "Who's going to walk me down the aisle?" I held her close and cried. I couldn't answer. I couldn't think that far ahead, couldn't imagine life without Rick.

Never before had I been so stunned and grief-stricken. Yet there was a voice deep inside me that assured me I would be okay, the same voice that had brought me comfort during the other tough times in my life. I knew I would have the strength to go on, and where that strength would come from. At the center of our marriage had been a love that superseded even our own. It was that love that would save me now.

In a way, that year seemed as long as all the years of marriage that preceded it. Grief has that way of seeming to bring time to a halt. Yet love never stands still. Love is always in motion. I have drawn on an even greater love than that which I shared with my husband. The unconditional love that comes from God, who has been there in the times I have wept and yelled, as well as the times

I have rested in Him and thanked Him for the years He gave me with Rick, the wonderful marriage we shared, and the beautiful children who keep us connected still. That love is never-ending.

Forever Love

Even though I walk
through the darkest valley,
I will fear no evil,
for you are with me....
Surely your goodness and love
will follow me
all the days of my life,
and I will dwell
in the house of the LORD forever.

PSALM 23:4, 6 NIV

Sincerely

BY SUE MONK KIDD

One late summer day far back in my childhood, Granddaddy and I picked the last of the blackberries along a country fence. Now and then he would hold a berry up to the sun and say, "This one should be eaten right away." With that I would whisk the berry from his fingers and gobble it up while he pretended great exasperation over losing it.

We picked and ate and laughed. Then all of a sudden I saw a wild sunflower growing alone among the briers. I picked it from the fence and, casting a look at Granddaddy, began to pluck away the petals. "Granddaddy loves me...loves me not...loves me...loves me not..." I was feeling the magic of a late summer kingdom, where blackberries and grandfathers and love would never end. "Loves me...loves me not...loves me..." Only one more petal. I stared at it, unable to say the final "loves me not." Somehow the magic had vanished. A few moments later I scratched my hand on a brier and burst into tears.

"That's a little scratch for such big tears," Granddaddy said. "Must have been a stinging thorn."

"Yessir, it was," I told him. But I wasn't only crying over the scratch. I was crying because there were no more petals. I didn't want it to end that way.

We got into his old black truck and jostled down the dirt road. Granddaddy peered through the windshield, looking side to side. Finally the truck stopped. Granddaddy stepped out, calling me to follow. There on the side of the road was a row of sunflowers! I reached for a blossom and once again plucked the petals from the brown button center and within moments I was able to exclaim, "Loves me!" as the last petal fell away. Granddaddy nodded and climbed back in the truck, his straw hat tilted over his glasses. I climbed in beside him, and the magic was once again with us. And away we went, laughing again, the red dust of summer billowing up behind us.

Of course, there was never any "interruption" of love between us that day. It existed only in the imagination of a little girl who still believed in the fancy of love-me-not flowers. But since then I've had lots of real "love-me-not" moments in my life—moments when I allow myself to believe that love has been denied me. Times when love for my husband or children or friends becomes overshadowed by anger, pride, bitterness, fear, or plain old apathy. But fortunately, I've learned that the presence of bad feelings doesn't have to mean the absence of love.

When these dark moments come, I am still tempted to sit quietly and nurse my little wounds, pridefully refusing to seek a brighter prospect. But, as my grandfather taught me, the secret to restoring the kingdom is never to let the "love-me-not" petal be the last one you touch. You keep on searching and trying until somehow, some way, you end with love.

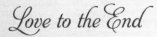

*Love keeps on growing
through life's joys and tears,
bringing a fragrance
that sweetens with years.*

ROY LESSIN

A Sea Change

BY MARK STUBBS

From the window of our hotel room in the fishing village of St. John's, Newfoundland, Canada, all I could see was a cold gray mist. But tomorrow—at last—fair weather was forecast, a fog-free break that would let us thread our rowboat through the ice-choked Grand Banks. Tomorrow we would launch *Pink Lady*.

Two years had passed since my last try at rowing across the Atlantic. In 2002 my team and I had failed when our rudder snapped during a storm. I'd designed the *Pink Lady*—named after an apple company that was one of our sponsors—with a rudder so strong the boat itself would break first. The commercial fishermen in St. John's had dubbed us "the four mad Englishmen," but they couldn't hear enough about our high-tech equipment, like the device for removing the salt from seawater to make it drinkable. Couldn't stop ragging us about the surfboard look of the boat, either. Thirty-three feet long and five feet wide, the little Lady was hydrodynamically designed for speed, her two rowing stations midway between the fore and aft cabins.

"Cabins?" The fishermen laughed, peering into the tiny enclosed spaces. "They look more like coffins!" It was the dark humor of men who knew what we would be up against in the North Atlantic.

True, the cabins were coffin-size. But they were the only cover we'd have in the seven weeks we figured it would take us to row the 2,100 miles from Canada to England. Each cabin was just big enough for a man to lie down in, plus hold the inflatable life raft and the "grab bag" filled with emergency supplies. Two men row, two rest, hour after hour, day and night.

We pushed off from St. John's on June 30, 2004, with visibility for dodging the "growlers"—icebergs that can roll without warning and crush a small boat.

On day seven we were safely past the Grand Banks and well ahead of schedule. Two years of physical and mental training were paying off. We were a true team now—Peter Bray, John Wills, Jonathan Gornall, and I—totally focused on maintaining a record pace. Twenty-nine times since 1898 men and women had tried to row across the Atlantic. Only ten attempts had succeeded. We figured we could beat the best time of fifty-five days by two weeks.

Through July contrary winds made us fight for each mile. But we maintained our speed, our spirits high. *Pink Lady*, we believed, could handle whatever the weather threw at us. Our GPS gave us our location, sun-powered batteries and satellite phones let us call our families daily.

My wife, Paula, was as excited about this race as I was. We'd been sweethearts since she was eleven and I was twelve, and we saw eye to eye on everything. Well, almost everything. Paula had begun attending church regularly. To my amazement, both our little girls, Victoria and Brianna, started going with her and loved it! I'd been bored with that stuff as a kid, scarcely setting foot in a church since our wedding. Stretching yourself, striving to exceed your best, taking on new challenges—that was my religion. As if my job as a firefighter weren't demanding enough, I was into marathon running, mountain biking, endurance swimming. And now the biggest test yet—this race across the Atlantic!

August 4, day thirty-six, we were only 300 miles from England, ahead even of our own prediction, and already picturing the celebration when we touched dockside at Falmouth. Paula and the girls would be there, and camera crews from all over.

Our satellite weather tracker called in with the daily report. Apparently an early hurricane called Alex was brewing—unusual on this date at this latitude. Not much to worry about. "Probably blow itself out over the Azores," he said.

"Hope it doesn't slow us down this close to the end," I grumbled.

Next day the tracker's voice on the phone was sober. Alex, it seemed, had fed on another storm and was picking up speed. "Better get ready for some heavy seas," he said.

By dawn next morning we were getting gale-force winds and rowing was impossible. We attached our safety lines as thirty-foot waves swept over the deck, drenching us in icy water. *Pink Lady* was performing beautifully, plunging from wave tip to trough with not a shiver in her.

When I called home I discovered that Paula and the girls were tracking the hurricane too. "We're praying," Paula said. Okay, if that made them feel better, but the *Lady* could handle anything.

At nightfall, winds hit hurricane force. In the hammering rain you couldn't tell air from water. John and Jonathan squeezed together into the aft cabin; Pete went forward. I was alone topside when I saw the outline of a wave five stories high roaring toward us. I dove for the forward cabin, pushed in beside Pete, and tugged the hatch shut. Locked in a pitch-black sardine can, we were tossed up, down, and sideways, hour after hour. Around two in the morning a monster wave lifted us up, up, still higher up. There was an explosive crack—and suddenly we were on our backs.

In that moment I had no idea the *Lady* would sink. Water streamed into the upside-down cabin. I groped for the hatch handle and pushed. Water flooded over us. I shoved through the hatchway into the angry ocean. Where was the surface? Lungs bursting, I clawed my way up to air. John, head bleeding, had managed to drag the emergency radio beacon from his cabin. In the flashes from its strobe I saw the *Pink Lady*, her two halves forming a 90-degree angle. Our lovely boat...gone.

In the lightning-like strobe flashes I saw that Jonathan was in trouble: his survival suit had filled with water and was dragging him under. Pete got to him, locked his arms around his suit, and squeezed till water gushed out around the neck.

The grab bag—all our safety stores—was still in the forward cabin. Pete signaled he was going to dive. After a tense wait he reappeared clutching the bag. He dove again, then surfaced with the life raft. Before we could inflate it, another monster wave slammed us. I was hurled yards from the boat. Hard as I swam, the wave sucked me farther away...farther...still farther. I couldn't see the strobe. Nothing but thundering water. I called out Paula's name. Brianna's. Victoria's. "I love you!" I shouted into the roaring blackness.

I love you. It was my own voice, calling out these words, but there was something else in the thrashing sea. Something bigger, deeper, wider than I could fathom. Something that seemed to engulf me, to swallow me whole....

Another great wave snatched me up and flung me forward. Next moment I found myself back beside the *Pink Lady*.

Pete was tugging at the ring on the life raft. With a hissing sound, the little rubber circle popped open. The four of us hauled ourselves aboard. We put out the raft's sea anchor, raised the canvas roof, and opened the grab bag. Everything was soaked. I took out the satellite phone. If it worked we had a chance. If not... I raised the antenna, threw the switch, and sighed with relief as a green light began to glow.

Within minutes we were talking to the Coast Guard in England. "We're adrift in a tiny rubber raft in battering winds and enormous waves," I reported. We had injuries too—John with a concussion, Jonathan with hypothermia.

Pete read out the coordinates from our GPS. "We'll check for ship traffic in the area," the Coast Guard said.

After an hour riding those roller-coaster seas, the Coast Guard reported a banana boat, the *Scandinavian Reefer*, riding out the storm fifty miles away. The Danish skipper agreed to attempt a rescue.

For six more hours we climbed and slid on that little raft, waves pummeling the roof. Pete and I took turns bailing and peering through the pounding rain for the boat. At last the vessel appeared. It took a half hour of fantastic seamanship to turn the ship around so our tiny raft would be in its lee. Waves swept us closer, then sucked us away with a hiss. One moment we'd be looking into the faces of the crew at the ship's rail, next moment staring at the barnacles on the bottom of her hull. The crewmen dropped a ladder over her side and fired a rescue line. It missed us. They tried again, and missed. At last the line came close enough for Pete to grab. Jonathan, in the worst condition, went up first. Swinging out over the ocean then banging against the side of the ship, he dragged himself up rung by rung until crewmen could grab him. John, weak from his head injury, went up next. Then I grabbed the swaying ladder and climbed up until strong hands dragged me over the rail. Trying to stand and thank them, I collapsed onto the pitching deck.

Several years have passed since that night, years that have transformed my life. *I love you*—the words I cried out in the roar of a hurricane—have become for me the reality undergirding the universe. Not my love, or Paula's love, or the love of strangers on a banana boat, but a love so all-encompassing it will take a lifetime to grasp. To know that love, to grow in it and serve it—at last I've found the ultimate challenge.

Ultimate Love

There is no limit to God's love.
It is without measure
and its depth cannot be sounded.

MOTHER TERESA

Home Team

BY MIKE SINGLETARY

Y ou need to know your priorities in life. As head coach of the San Francisco 49ers, that's probably the most important message I deliver to my players, especially the younger ones. Focus on what's truly meaningful, I urge them. I'm a guy who wears his emotions on his sleeve, so when I say these things, my players know I speak from the heart. What they don't know is that I learned that lesson the hard way. They weren't there in Chicago the night of the banquet in my honor—one of the greatest moments of my career as a player, and the lowest point of my personal life.

I'd played my entire NFL career with the Chicago Bears. In the 1985 season I'd helped lead the team to a victory in the Super Bowl. Chicago fans always appreciated me, and this night in 1989 would make it official. All the goals I'd set at age twelve had come true. I was being honored in my adopted city as the best defensive player in the league.

You can imagine what the night was like. People approached my table throughout the evening. "Congratulations, Mike," they'd say, pushing between my wife, Kim, and me. They'd pay me a ton of compliments, and then turn to Kim and say, "Oh, you're so lucky to be married to him."

I figured, if ever I could make Kim proud, this would be the time. "This is our night, honey," I said. Kim said nothing. We barely spoke through dinner. Driving home, Kim didn't say a word. Her eyes said it all.

How did it ever get to this? I wondered. Kim is the only woman I've ever loved. I thought back to the night we met—in the Baylor University library, when we were sophomores. I was already well known on campus as a football player. But off the field I wasn't nearly so confident. I'd seen Kim around but couldn't work up the nerve to approach her. I couldn't believe it when she walked up to me. "Can you help me with my math?" she asked. I wasn't very good at math, but I told her I was. Afterward, I walked her back to her dorm. We talked about a million things—family, faith, our hopes, our dreams. *Man*, I thought, as I returned to my dorm, *she doesn't care that I'm a football player. Kim's the first girl I've met where I can just be myself.*

A few days later we went on our first date. I never did believe in beating around the bush. "I'm going to marry you someday," I said.

The next few months were heaven. For me, at least. I felt lucky to be around Kim. I thought she felt the same. Turns out she didn't. We were a couple, but we didn't spend much time together. Not as much as she wanted. Most of my hours were spent on the field, or studying. One day she cornered me. "Where do I stand with you?" she asked.

"I truly love you," I said. But she wasn't satisfied.

Where to begin? I took Kim to a campus coffee shop and found a quiet corner. I was twelve when my parents divorced. I took it hard. I lost all my desire, all my motivation. Even for football, which I loved. I just wanted to get by. I told Kim I probably wouldn't have cared about college, almost certainly wouldn't have amounted to anything. Until my mother talked some sense into me.

"Nobody gets life handed to them," Mom told me. "Life is getting beat up and getting back on your feet. It takes willpower and hard work and focus."

I told Kim it was the greatest motivational speech I'd ever heard, better than any delivered by a football coach. It turned my attitude right around. I went straight to my room and wrote out a vision statement. My goals, I decided, were to earn a college football scholarship, to become an All-American player, to earn my degree, to get drafted by an NFL team, to become an All-Pro player, to buy Mom a home, to play in the Super Bowl, and to own my own business. "I became a totally goal-oriented person," I told Kim. Single-minded, you might say. A fitting description for a guy named Singletary.

"There's something missing from your list, Mike," she said, touching my hand. "Love."

I told Kim the truth: nothing was going to keep me from going for my goals, for getting where I wanted to go. That even included my relationships.

A lot of women would have said good-bye right then. But Kim knew the sincerity of my heart. Eventually, she believed, a wife and family would rate at the top of my list.

But they never did. There was always something else that demanded my attention. In 1981 the Bears drafted me and I achieved one of my main goals. I thought things would get easier. They didn't. Most nights I fell asleep studying the team's playbook. I was determined to be the best. Kim moved back to Detroit, where her family lived. I can't tell you how much I missed her. My heart ached. Did I ask her to move back and marry me? No. It was more important to establish myself in the league.

That took three years. I made All-Pro and felt things were falling into place for me. I called Kim. "I'm ready for you now," I said. "I'm ready to give you the attention you deserve." That summer we married. The next year we had the first of our seven children.

I loved being with Kim. But things kept cutting into my time with her and our children. "Nothing has changed," she complained one night. "You come home, and even at dinner your attention wanders. I know your mind is on football." I couldn't argue. I was named team captain. I'd wolf down dinner then spend the rest of the night watching film of the next week's opponent and phoning teammates to make sure they were doing the same.

I thought I was succeeding in life. The truth is, I wasn't paying enough attention to the most important thing of all—Kim and the kids. But I didn't realize how dissatisfied Kim was until that night at the banquet. Our marriage had reached a crisis. *Mike, you better figure this out*, I thought. *You better fix this*.

Kim marched upstairs with barely a good night. I went into the den, grabbed a notebook, and followed her into the bedroom. I felt like I did the night I met her: unsure of myself, deathly afraid I'd blow it. *I love this woman. I can't bear the idea of losing her*, I thought. I sat down on the edge of the bed with notebook in hand. I was going to make a list, just like I did when I was twelve. "I need to know," I said. "Am I the kind of husband that you need? How do I treat you? What am I doing that needs fixing?"

"Let me think about it for a while," Kim said.

Every time I saw her over the next few days, I asked if she had an answer yet. I wanted to make my list, set my goals.

One morning at the kitchen table Kim laid it all out for me. My divided attention, leaving the hard work of parenting up to her, tending to my career first at the expense of all else. "You have to be here for us, with us. With me. This family has to come before football."

It was pretty tough to hear—that a man so wrapped up in success could fail in his wife's eyes. It humbled me. I promised to do better. But old habits die slow. Football is what defined me. One night Kim and I got into a terrible argument. I can't even remember what it was about. As usual, I didn't quit until

I had won. She marched upstairs, as frustrated as I'd ever seen her, and slammed the door. *What have I actually won?* I thought.

I sat down in the den. This time I reached for the Bible, thinking it would calm me. Flipping through the pages, I came across 1 Corinthians 13—the love chapter. "Love is not boastful, not proud, not self-seeking." And it struck me—I was all of those things. I kept reading. "But love never fails. Love is patient, love is kind. It is not easily angered." I thought back again to my first date with Kim. She liked me for who I was, not because I was a football player. I didn't have to prove anything to her except my love.

I snapped the Bible closed and took it upstairs with me. It was 2:00 a.m. Kim rolled over drowsily in bed.

"Kim, read this," I said.

"You read it."

I did. And when I finished I said to her, "You're my number-one priority. You and the kids. From this day forward that's how I'm going to love you."

It took me five years of marriage, but I finally figured out what's really important in life. Football is a big part of who I am. But not as big as my wife and kids, in terms of who I am off the field—a man of God and a family man.

By the way, it was Kim who suggested that I go into coaching eleven years after I retired as a player in 1992. I love being the head coach of the San Francisco 49ers. But if Kim told me to leave the 49ers tomorrow, that would be it. After all these years, I finally got my list straightened out.

Love's Priority

Love creates a special world for two people. Everything within it is guarded and preserved by commitment, faithfulness, and trust. Everything about it is enriched and endeared by kindness, gentleness, and care.

Grandpa, I Can Still Hear You

BY GREGORY G. HEYWORTH

One day right after my eleventh birthday, I almost stopped believing in God. I recall vividly that early April morning. The sun was just peeping over the edge of Long Island Sound, and the breeze blew briskly over the whitecaps. I shivered in that breeze and dug my sneakered feet into the sand, and bit my lips to keep from crying with loneliness. We had just finished moving into our new house the night before, and I was trying to accustom myself to this new world a hundred miles away from my friends in the foothills of the Berkshire Mountains. Most of all, I was trying to learn to live in a world without my dog Duffy.

His official name was McDuff, and his ancestry was uncertain, although some hound and some pointer had shaped his face. Sometimes he would even point. He would tremble for a moment and look intense, and then his tail would jerk upright and his body would stiffen, while a cabbage butterfly flapped past the serious expression on his muzzle.

Moving far away wouldn't have been so bad with Duffy for company. I imagined him racing across the beach and tripping over his own big feet. Suddenly, biting my lip didn't help anymore, and I found myself crying even though I was now eleven years old.

It wasn't as if Duffy had died. That might have been easier to bear somehow. It was that he had just disappeared the day before we moved to the shoreline down by my grandparents' house. Maybe all the boxes and the strangers around had confused him, and he had run farther than he had intended. Maybe he had been hit by a truck and lay suffering in a ditch. Maybe dognappers had caught him. He would be easy to steal, he was so friendly.

I had prayed hard for Duffy's return the night he disappeared. In the morning, I ran down and flung open the front door, knowing that Duffy would be sitting on the porch eager for his breakfast. But he wasn't there. All morning I waited without giving up hope, praying silently for his return. After lunch, the movers came. They were big, efficient men, and it seemed as if the van was filled in no time at all, and our empty house remained furnished only with echoes and memories.

We called the dog warden and the state police and all the neighbors before we left. My mom consoled me, saying that one of them was sure to find Duffy, and that they all had our new address and phone number. But her consolation didn't help me very much. I fell asleep crying in my new room, and when I awoke, I felt that I didn't believe in God anymore.

The sand and water spread out endlessly around me, and I shivered, not just from the cool breeze on my bare legs, but with an inner chill—the chill of abandonment and alienation. At that moment I heard the tread of firm, unhurried footsteps approaching me across the sand. I looked up and saw Grandpa settle down on a big rock nearby. He smiled and called me to him. Hastily I sniffed and wiped my eyes.

Grandpa didn't seem to notice that I'd been crying. At least he didn't say anything about it at the time. Instead he began to talk about the beach. He pointed to Duck Island on the horizon and told me about the great fishing there when the stripers were running.

Soon I felt calm enough to confide in him.

"How can there be a God," I exclaimed, "if I prayed and prayed, and Duffy still didn't come back? And even if He exists, what kind of God is it that doesn't even care a little bit about how I feel?"

I remember how Grandpa put his gnarled, strong hand on my shoulder, gave me a gentle squeeze, and began speaking again.

"Boy," he said, "God never abandoned you. You're feeling so awful because you've just abandoned Him. You've got to love God for what He is, not for what He gives, because God loves you for what you are. Yes, He loves you personally, and knows you, and sees you, just as He knows, and loves, and sees, and hears that sea gull overhead, and the fish under those waves. And God, in His mysterious way, determines what's right for you, and that sea gull, and that fish, and for Duffy too.

"Do you love your mom and dad just because they give you gifts? Would you stop loving them if they didn't get you all those gifts? That would be a pretty selfish, hollow kind of love, and not a warm, real love. Sure you feel bad about losing Duffy, but you feel even worse about losing your faith in God. That empty pain inside is your spirit hungering to be fed with the love of the Lord, to drink at the well of faith. God never abandons anybody, boy. For your own sake, don't you abandon Him."

Despite the years that have passed, I remember his words exactly as he said them, his voice blending with the splash of the water, rolling with the waves, punctuated by the cry of an occasional sea gull. Somehow all those sounds penetrated past my pain, into the hollow within me, and filled me with a great affirmation of the divine Presence. With a breath of relief, I felt the pain depart.

The following day, the dog warden called long distance to tell us that he'd checked our old house and found Duffy on the porch, smiling and wagging his tail, and ravenously hungry. That, however, was not the end of this adventure.

The ending came a few years later with Grandpa's death. Again I found myself on the now-familiar beach. Duffy was with me. His muzzle was graying, and he didn't race about as much as he used to. He ran and then pointed, and turned to see if I was watching. But I barely saw him. Instead, in the wind and in the rolling, grating sound of the waves, I heard again my grandfather's voice, and his wisdom reaffirmed my faith.

"God never abandons anybody, boy. For your own sake, don't you ever abandon Him."

I called to Duffy, and together we moved slowly home.

Faithful Love

Love the LORD your God, listen to his voice,
and hold fast to him. For the LORD is your life....
The LORD your God goes with you;
he will never leave you nor forsake you.

DEUTERONOMY 30:20; 31:6 NIV

The Man I Married

BY KIM PRIDGEON

Michael looked up at me from his wheelchair. We were ready to move him from the hospital to the rehabilitation center. "Doing all right, sweetie?" I asked, letting my hand rest on his shoulder. He still felt so solid, so strong.

Michael nodded. "Thank you, Kimberly," he said, his voice hoarse from the days he'd spent with a ventilator tube snaked down his throat. Funny, he'd called me Kim ever since we met in college, but I didn't mind. I was just grateful God had given me my husband back.

Only two and a half weeks earlier, on June 27, 1997, Michael had been airlifted to the hospital, unconscious. The lift he was riding at the manufacturing plant where he was an electrical engineer collapsed. He hit the concrete floor headfirst. Traumatic brain injury, the doctors said—so severe they didn't expect him to make it through the night. *Lord, he has to!* I prayed desperately, clutching a photo of Michael and me with our two-year-old, Amanda. *We have a little girl at home and another baby on the way. Don't let him die.*

As if he heard my prayer, Michael clung to life that night. And the next. Doctors warned me: even if he did regain consciousness, it wasn't likely he'd regain normal brain function. Then, miraculously, Michael came to. "Kimberly," he rasped. He sounded so different from the day we'd exchanged our wedding vows eight years earlier, but he knew me!

Now he was being moved to a rehab center for brain-injured patients. There the therapists reminded me of how much Michael had to relearn. Basic skills—feeding himself, dressing, brushing his teeth, walking. "Don't expect your husband to be the man you knew, Mrs. Pridgeon. He won't be for a long time. Maybe not ever."

How could Michael no longer be the person God had brought into my life? It was his body, his brain, that had been injured. Surely not his spirit. Not his faith. Not the qualities that I'd fallen in love with.

The rehab staff did some benchmark tests for brain function. They put everyday objects—a coin, a paper clip, a pencil—on a table in front of Michael. Could he show us what they were used for?

Michael picked up the coin, put it in his mouth, and tried to eat it. *Lord, You brought my husband back from the brink of death... but have I lost him anyway?*

The neurologist took me aside. "I have to be honest, Mrs. Pridgeon. Only one in twenty-five people with your husband's level of brain injury is able to return to his job. Still, the brain can always surprise us. There's so much we don't know about how it works. Don't give up hope."

I tried not to. It was hard, though, seeing Michael struggle day after day to master the simplest tasks. He was trying his best. What if that wasn't enough?

One afternoon I watched Michael play dominoes, resisting the urge to show him how to do it. His look of concentration made me think of our study dates back in college. We didn't have money to go out, so a lot of times we'd just do our homework together, savoring the simple pleasure of being with each other. If only things could be that uncomplicated now...

All of sudden Michael turned to me and asked, "Are you going to leave me?"

The question was as absurd as his response to the coin. Michael had always been strong. He wasn't into talking about his feelings, but when it came to showing his faith, his commitment to me, he never hesitated. On the one-year anniversary of our first date he'd festooned my room with 144 hearts he'd cut out of paper and decorated. He loved me that much, and he wanted me to know.

Now Michael grasped the gravity of his situation enough to pose that heartbreaking question. Was this a sign that he wasn't completely lost to me?

"Michael," I said, taking his hand, "when I said 'I do,' it meant forever. I love you."

Tears filled his eyes. He pulled me closer and, for the first time since the accident, held me in his arms.

His occupational therapist told me that the brain responds to stimulation, and the guys from Michael's plant took it upon themselves to provide it. At first they quizzed him on basic concepts. Basic to engineers, anyway; I had no idea what they were talking about. With each visit, the questions grew more technical until one day I overheard Michael say, "Wait, here's what you need to do..." and launched into a detailed explanation. Amazing!

In mid-August, just six weeks after the accident, Michael came home. With this warning: "We don't know how he's going to react," the doctor said. "He may find it stressful, and under stress, brain-injured people behave unpredictably." I hid all the sharp objects and medications. What if he found them and hurt himself? At the rehab center Michael couldn't sleep through the night. The staff would find him roaming the corridors at all hours. What if he wandered out of the house while I was asleep? He and Amanda acted tentative, as if they didn't know each other anymore. What if he couldn't reconnect with her?

That first night Michael snuggled against me in bed. How I'd longed to feel his body next to mine again! I lay awake watching his chest rise and fall in the peaceful, even rhythm of sleep. *God, I want to believe Michael's place is with me. You've brought us this far. Give us the strength to face whatever lies ahead.*

Michael still looked like the man I married, but in many ways he was like an overgrown child, and more dependent on me than Amanda was. He'd trail me around the house while I did the chores. I couldn't stay on the phone without him tugging on my sleeve. He'd blurt out whatever he was thinking, even if it wasn't appropriate, like at church or restaurants, or in front of Amanda.

Just before our second daughter was born in November, I had a talk with Michael. "The new baby's going to need a lot from me," I said. "When I'm busy, you'll have to look after Amanda."

Michael surprised me—and himself—by rising to the challenge. He and Amanda bonded again. He was lost, though, when it came to Ashley, our new baby. Her needs, her moods, were a mystery to him. He didn't understand why my attention couldn't be constantly focused on him.

I got fed up. At my parents' house for Christmas, exhausted from all the holiday preparations, I dragged myself to the bathroom. Michael followed right after me.

"Can't you give me a break for once?" I snapped. "Sometimes I think maybe we should part ways if we can't figure out how to make things between us work better."

"I'm sorry, Kim," Michael said. "I just want us to be together."

"Oh, Michael," I sighed, "me too."

We started going to counseling together. Michael told me he wanted to go back to work in February. I hesitated. I needed all the help I could get at home. But his doctors and our counselor thought providing for us might help him regain his confidence as a husband and father.

Working again did make him feel better about himself. Still, I kept looking after everyone at home. The months wore on, and

I wore out. Some nights I'd lie awake next to Michael and weep silently. *Lord, You know I'm committed to our marriage. Except now I need more from Michael.* But how could I ask that after all he'd been through?

That summer I finally poured everything out to our counselor. "You trust God to share both your joys and your burdens," she said. "Give the man He joined you with a chance to do the same. Let your husband know what you need from him."

One night I sat down with Michael. "It's time for me to stop being your caregiver and start being your wife again," I said. "I want to do what it takes to make our marriage work. Do you?"

"I do, Kim," Michael said. "I'll do anything. I don't want to make your life hard."

He took my hand and once more I looked into his eyes as I had the day he asked if I would leave him. How hard, how sad, would my life have been if God hadn't given me back Michael? And our children...they had their father. I'd never felt more grateful. Yet something had to change. I was ready to accept that my husband would never be quite the same person he was before the accident. Neither of us was. But he was still the man whom God meant for me, still the man I loved with all my heart. That hadn't changed.

"Michael," I whispered, stroking his cheek, "even if life is hard sometimes, I love you no matter what."

Counseling has helped us renew our commitment to each other. Strangely, what's sometimes embarrassing in public—Michael's post-accident propensity to share all his thoughts and emotions, his incredible sensitivity to my feelings—has turned out to be an enormous blessing when it comes to our relationship. He's so willing to talk about everything.

Several years have passed since the accident, and Michael and I are not the same people we were when we met. We're stronger. Stronger in our commitment and our love—for God and each other. Especially now that we've been blessed with our third child, Allison.

Not long ago Michael came home from work, and before I even said a word, he could tell I'd had a bad day. "I'll be right back," he said. Ten minutes later I heard his car pull into the driveway again. "I think you might need these, sweetie," he said, and whisked out a big bunch of carnations. Pink, my favorite color.

Michael's short-term memory will never be what it used to, and I have to keep prodding him to help around the house. Some things, though, he's always reminding me of—like how much he loves me. And how we are meant to be together.

Meant to Be

Love isn't the tingly sensation you feel
when you hold someone's hand for the first time....
True, lasting love comes after struggling together
through the hard times, remembering the good
times, and having faith that God will
help you over one more hill together.

RHONDA S. HOGAN

A Field of Jonquils

BY JAN LaROSA

I got my first job at the concession stand at the Golf Mill Theater in Niles, Illinois. Mom worked there too, selling tickets, and one of the fringe benefits was that we could see any movie for free. One night after our shifts, we stayed for the late show: *Doctor Zhivago*—all three hours of it. I don't think I'd ever seen anything more romantic. Here was the story of the dark-eyed Doctor Zhivago (dashing Omar Sharif) and his love for the nurse Lara (gorgeous Julie Christie) set against the backdrop of the Russian Revolution— wrenching shots of soldiers being treated by Zhivago and Lara, and heart-stopping scenes of revolutionaries in the Moscow streets. We saw the glamour of Russian society with their rich sables and silks, especially a ravishing red dress worn by Julie Christie.

But the scene that took our breath away came near the end when Zhivago made a brutal trek across an icy landscape to meet his beloved Lara again. All at once the snows are gone and the screen melts into a field of jonquils fluttering in the breeze. Lara's theme, the song I came to know as "Somewhere My Love," swoops in, and you know that for all the misery the couple has faced and all the sorrow still ahead, their love will survive. Love would always triumph over the dark forces of history.

After that my heart would stir every time the strains of Lara's theme would reach the candy counter. From my perch I could picture Julie Christie in her fur hat with her love, Omar Sharif. And I could see the jonquils! One night Mom came by. "It's break time," she said. "Come with me." We climbed the stairs and stood in the doorway. I looked to the screen and there they were—a whole field of yellow flowers swaying to Lara's theme. For the rest of the long run, Mom and I took our breaks so we could watch that one moment in *Doctor Zhivago* when the snows melt and spring bursts through. Things were hard at home. Money was tight and we ate a lot of sandwiches, but that shared moment of springtime in the back of the theater gave us hope. We had our love for each other and knew that God loved us too. We would get through—and we did.

For Mom's birthday I bought her the soundtrack to *Doctor Zhivago*, and long after the movie stopped playing at the Golf Mill Theater, she'd listen to it. Time and again I'd find her sitting next to the stereo, murmuring the words of the song. We watched the movie too whenever it turned up on TV, the two of us waiting for the golden jonquils in the field.

Years later Mom was in the hospital, fighting an illness she wouldn't survive. Sitting by her bedside, I searched for words of comfort. As her breathing slowed I hummed the song we both loved. Then I whispered: "The breeze is warm and gentle, the snows are gone and the jonquils are swaying, extending as far as the eye can see...."

Circle of Love

A mother's love is like a circle,
it has no beginning and no ending.
It keeps going around and around
ever expanding, touching everyone
who comes in contact with it.
Engulfing them like the morning's mist,
warming them like the noontime sun,
and covering them like
a blanket of evening stars.

ART URBAN

The Stranger My Daughter Married

BY ANSON REYNOLDS

L ike many men, I adored my daughter. That Tory was my pet was a family fact; that she had me wound around her little finger was a family joke.

Tory was always "baby" to me. That was why I was stunned the night she announced that she was going to get married: I had not realized how the years had flown.

"Who's the man?" I asked.

"Walter, of course," she said.

I looked at my wife and challenged, "You don't seem surprised."

Doris was smiling. "I've seen this coming for months."

"I didn't even know Walter was a serious contender," I admitted. I had blinded myself, I suppose, to the probability that anybody would be. Walter was almost a stranger to me. "He teaches school, doesn't he?"

"Oh, Dad!" Tory said with happy impatience. "Yes, he teaches school—at the same place I do, and you know it."

"Well," I said, "a man can't support a wife on that salary."

"I'll continue working," Tory said. "I'll have to, to help pay for Walter's studies for his doctorate. Anyway, I want to work."

To me it seemed so foolish to rush. "A man shouldn't expect his wife to support him," I said testily.

Doris was perturbed; her face showed it but her voice was calm. "Kids are different these days," she said.

"That's the point," I said. "They're just kids." I got up and left the room.

Tory called after me, teasing, "He's going to ask you tomorrow night and you'd better say yes."

I heard Doris assure, "He will."

I did, but only because I could not say no to Tory. And yet I was sure it was a mistake.

Right off, the trouble started. To save them money, I suggested that they live with us, but Walter refused. They took a small furnished flat in a failing part of town, and when Doris and I visited them for dinner and I saw Tory struggling with ancient kitchen equipment, I sickened for her. She looked tired.

"You shouldn't be making that miserable bus trip back and forth to school every day," I said. "It must exhaust you. Let me get you a car." To placate Walter's pride, I added, "Just an old one."

Walter said, "You've spoiled her enough, Dad." I always winced when he called me Dad.

Tory said, "I don't mind the trip. Going, I prepare my classes; coming back, I grade papers. I couldn't do either driving a car."

She's defending him, I told myself, and I resented him for embarrassing her into it. With time, I found I resented everything about him—his attitudes, his open influence on Tory. When he left for the summer session at the university, I was relieved to be rid of him, and I was startled when Tory said she would follow him as soon as he found an inexpensive place for them to live. A few weeks later Tory wrote that she had taken a job as a shopclerk; I was furious.

Shortly before Christmas, Tory stopped by alone on a Saturday afternoon and announced that she was pregnant. Impulsively, I exclaimed, "How thoughtless of Walter."

"Of Walter?" she said, laughing. "I was a party to this too!"

I rejected her joke. "It's bad enough that he expects you to support him," I said. "He shouldn't burden you with children on top of it." And I walked out of the room. That Christmas, for the first time in over twenty years, Tory was not with us: she and Walter went to spend the holidays with friends, Walter's friends. I could scarcely bring myself to speak to him after that.

In May, Tory lost her baby and we almost lost Tory. I was sure that if Tory had had proper rest and care the tragedy wouldn't have happened. "This settles it," I told her. "You're coming back home and you're going to stay there. This whole thing has been a mistake."

She looked at me for a moment with a chilly evenness, then all she said was, "I don't think we ought to see each other for a while, Dad." And she turned her face away from me.

I stalked out of the hospital with a hatred raging in me, determined that if I could not make Tory see her mistake I would settle it with Walter. I sped to his school and parked across the street, waiting for him. I had no idea what I would do, but somehow I had to free all of us from that man. When I saw him come out of the building and head toward the bus stop, I left my car and hurried to him. I did not see the car that roared down at me.

Doris was holding my hand when I regained consciousness in the hospital and saw the troubled concern on her face. I became aware that my legs were in traction and my head was bandaged. To comfort Doris, I said, "I'll be all right."

She shook her head. "You'll heal, but you won't be all right. Dear, what have you done to yourself? I've heard that resentment could kill a person, but I thought you had more sense." There was a softness in her tone despite the hardness of her words. "Why won't you let Tory and Walter be happy?"

"Tory isn't happy," I said.

"Has she told you that?"

"She doesn't have to. I know my own daughter."

"Do you?" Doris asked. "Have you any idea how often she's told me she wished you'd let her grow up? You never have."

I tried to shake my head and felt a stab of pain. "I won't have it."

Tears filled Doris's eyes. "And you let resentment blind you so much that you walk in front of a car. You're destroying yourself. That isn't like you."

I had no more words. The nurse came in and said I must rest. Doris took her hand from mine. "I'll go down to the chapel and pray," she said. "I can't get through to you anymore; maybe God can."

A small storm boiled in me. I was annoyed that I should be a matter for prayer. I always had considered myself a religious man and I could not see that what I was doing now might be evil. Couldn't my resentment be justified? I thought of resentment I had seen in others and tried to understand it—the salesman in my office who resented the success of others, the secretary who so resented working late that she invariably botched up the job, the old-timer in my club who resented the congenial newcomer who was elected president.

I began to feel uneasy. I began to see that those who had expressed resentment had all acted against love. I suddenly saw in them what I began to sense in myself—the self-inflicted wounds of a shattered pride that seeks to heal itself by lashing out at others who innocently were the occasion of it. In my own case, I found myself facing the bitter fact that the reason I had resented Walter was that I feared Tory's love for him made her love me less and I could not stand that. Yet I knew I had not loved Doris less when Tory came; in fact, I seemed able to love more.

Wasn't this always true of God-sent love? Couldn't it be true for Tory, when Walter came along? In my resentment, I had not given her the chance to show it. I would not let myself see that new love can make old loves deeper, richer.

I thought of Doris, praying in the chapel. So often over the years we had prayed together in so many places. Our prayers were like a private language our united hearts spoke to God. Thinking this, I realized how much, these past months, my heart had grown spiritually silent. I could not remember when I had prayed last. Resentment had so robbed me of the ability to love that I had even lost the faculty of loving God through prayer.

This truth gave me fresh pain, for I saw that not only had I become separated from my wife and my daughter but, worse, I had become separated from God, who had given me both. How close I had come to losing all three.

The nurse leaned over and peered into my face. "You're crying," she said. "Is the pain bad? The doctor said I could give you a sedative if you wanted it."

"No, I'll be all right," I said. "Will you let my wife in when she comes from the chapel? I want to tell her her prayers have been answered."

A Prayer for Love

O God, creator of light:
at the rising of Your sun this morning,
let the greatest of all lights, Your love,
rise like the sun within our hearts.

ARMENIAN PRAYER

The Loner

BY ABBY SUSAN PEOPLES

The shadows in the canyon were already deepening to purple by the time my friend David and I left the biting cold of the mountain river to climb back up the ridge to the mesa above, where we'd stashed our heavy hiking gear. Wearing only T-shirts and jeans, we had earlier descended a gentler slope to one side, drawn by the sight of that idyllic valley so far below. Now, looking up from the dusky canyon floor toward the looming cliff face, still rimmed at the top in gold from the rays of the setting sun, we decided to avoid the easier path and to climb straight up into the light.

The challenge suited me. I was proud of my strong, lean body—proud of my "toughness," my independence.

As we started the climb, I glanced toward David, whom I had met just a couple of weeks before. I had to admire his own lean strength as he nimbly scaled that rocky wall. I felt I could like him very much if I would choose to do so, but I'd fought against the idea—was still fighting it. Any kind of closeness to another human being seemed to me to be a dangerous thing. To invite a person to come near meant also to invite emotional pain, and that I could do without. I'd watched my parents suffer through a divorce when I'd been a child, and I hadn't liked what the stress did to them, or to me. I'd decided to keep everyone at a distance, surround myself by an invisible wall. I would shut out all emotion and become totally self-sufficient.

I'd succeeded in that goal. After growing up and leaving home, I'd held several different jobs, one of them as manager of a restaurant. That, too, had been a challenge, but I'd liked being in charge of a business. Just as I liked being in charge of my own life and destiny, climbing up this cliff.

As the way grew steeper, edging toward vertical, I constantly tested the stability of the rocks before trusting them with my weight. Several times I found a rock to be loose and I searched for a different handhold or foothold before moving higher. Soon I had ascended almost two hundred feet. I glanced again toward David, seeing that he was off to one side and a little higher than I. We had only thirty or so more feet to go before reaching the top.

And then it happened. I hooked my fingers around the edge of a shelf of rock above me that I'd thought was secure, only to have it suddenly give way. With a feeling of disbelief, as though everything had gone into slow motion, I lost my balance and dropped into space, followed by a huge chunk of ledge. I heard David scream, "My God, oh my God!"

God was Someone else I'd shut out of my life. All my growing years I had attended a strict religious school where the teachers described God as an angry, vengeful Being who would send me to hell for my sins. I didn't like that God, and I'd decided I wanted no part of Him. I'd go it alone, assuming responsibility for my own actions, instead of cowering in fear before some cruel, mythical judge.

And so, even in my present extremity, falling toward death, I did not call on God. But David continued to cry out; not in prayer, but in an agonized, involuntary repetition of the name.

Now occurred, in sequence, several events so incredible that I find them hard to believe to this day. I had fallen with my face toward the cliff, but now my body flipped around in midair, like a cat's, so that I was facing outward. Consequently, when my feet twice touched slight protrusions in the cliff's surface, I was tilted backward, toward the cliff face, instead of being catapulted farther into space. Then my feet landed on a small ledge, barely wide enough for one person, and the only ledge on that whole cliff between me and the ground. A few inches to either side, and I would have fallen past it. Sliding between two large cacti, I came to a halt with my legs hanging over the ledge. In one more second, I should have been crushed by the falling shelf of rock, which was several cubic feet in size. Instead, just before it would have hit me, it veered inexplicably to the right, grazing my shoulder and arm as it roared past.

I hung there in a daze, clutching at my narrow perch with my left hand while watching that boulder fall away toward the canyon floor 150 feet below. David came scrambling back down the cliff, frantically calling out to me. As he drew near, I heard him breathe, "Thank God, you're alive!" And then his voice changed as he groaned, "Susan—your leg..."

As yet, I felt no pain. Consequently, it was with amazement that I viewed my shattered left leg. Through the tattered remnants of my jeans, I saw three holes in the flesh of my lower leg from which broken bones protruded. My foot hung twisted around at an odd angle, like the leg of a discarded doll. I turned my head away, only to see that the inside of my right arm had been sliced completely open, elbow to wrist, exposing ripped ligaments and tendons, and a rubbery length of artery—scratched but not severed—pulsing deep inside the gaping wound.

I looked back toward David and saw that he had turned dead-white. He asked me if I thought my spine was damaged. I took mental inventory of my body, trying to determine if I had internal injuries, but I just couldn't tell. At last David said, "I don't dare try to get you off this cliff alone. I'm going to have to leave you and go for help."

I knew he was right. But the initial shock that had numbed me was beginning to wear off. I was suddenly hit by pain so devastating it froze my breath.

"Hurry—just hurry," I gasped.

He scrambled away at an angle up the ridge, heading toward the mesa and the trail that would take him out of these rugged Sangre de Cristo mountains (a Spanish name meaning "Blood of Christ") toward the jeep road, far away, where we'd left our four-wheel-drive pickup truck. I knew that the nearest hospital had to be in Española, New Mexico, about twenty miles away. I also knew it would take hours for a rescue crew to hike in with a litter. The light faded fast, taking with it the last heat from the sun. I began to shiver in my thin shirt, for September nights in the high country get very cold. In the distance I heard the rumbling thunder of an approaching storm.

As the minutes passed, the pain grew in intensity until I felt consumed by it. The storm arrived, bringing darkness and an icy rain. The surface of the ledge became slick with water and mud, so that I had to concentrate all my strength in my left arm, trying to hold on.

My mind whirled with giddiness. It would be so easy to let go and slip into that void. To die, and end the pain.

I'd recently read a book called *Life After Life* in which people who had been declared clinically dead returned to life with stories about having met a sentient light filled with love. I didn't know if such a Being existed. But if it did, it couldn't be that hateful personage called "God."

I wanted to pray to that light, but I didn't know what to call it. Finally, I did call it God, for want of a better name. I prayed for help to arrive, and for the strength to hold on until then. I said I was frightened. I said I didn't want to be alone.

And He came.

I saw no light. I heard no voice. All I can tell you is that suddenly, beside me on that ledge, there was a Presence. A Presence filled with warmth and love. I could feel strength pouring into me from that Presence, joining with, and energizing, my own fading will.

The thoughts in my mind were in my own voice, but they said, *Hold on. You can make it. You are not alone. Help will come.*

The comfort I felt in this Presence is indescribable. Whenever I would begin to fade out, something would snap me awake once more and I would discover just enough willpower left in me to pull away from the edge.

But I wanted more. I wanted the touch of a human hand. All these years, I had kept people away. Now, suspended in air on this cold cliff, crying out in pain with almost every breath, I longed desperately for someone to hold me, to talk to me, to distract me from the prison of agony my body had become.

Time flowed into a meaningless blur. And then, between my cries, I heard someone, faint and far away, calling my name. Peering down into the darkness, I saw a tiny light bobbing along the canyon floor.

I called to that light, and the light answered. I saw it veer toward me and proceed, slowly but surely, up the cliff. A face came into view over the side of the ledge, eerily white in the flashlight's glow.

It was a child. A boy about twelve or thirteen years old. I thought for a moment that I was hallucinating. But the boy scrambled up beside me on the slippery ledge. He carefully set the flashlight down in a depression in the rocks. And then he took a folded blanket from his shoulder and draped it over me, shielding me from the rain.

"Who are you?" I whispered.

"I'm Michael," he replied.

He was real. The touch of his small, dirt-roughened hands told me that. He explained that David, frantically looking for a phone, had shown up at the door of Michael's house, outside the canyon. But Mr. Browne, Michael's father, had no phone and was too ill to help with any kind of rescue effort. After hastily telling the Brownes about the accident, David had rushed away, heading once more down the mountain in his search for help.

"I thought you might be cold," Michael said, "so I came to find you."

He said he'd ridden his dirt bike until the brush got too thick. Then he'd hiked on into the canyon, and at last he'd heard my cries.

He asked what he could do for me, and I suggested that he elevate my injured arm. Surprisingly, my wounds had clotted soon after the accident, so I was no longer bleeding profusely; but elevating the arm seemed to help ease the pain. However, as we shifted on the ledge, I once more slipped toward the edge. Michael quickly grabbed my shoulders and held on, stopping my fall. After he had maneuvered me back to relative safety, he continued to hang on to me, while assuring me that the rescuers would arrive soon. He made me talk in order to keep me awake. Each time I started to slide forward on the slick surface of the ledge, Michael tightened his hold, dragging me back again. He was so determined to save me that I am convinced, had I actually gone over the edge, he would not have released his hold, but would have fallen with me to his own death.

As my mind wandered, I got to thinking that Michael might be a guardian angel. But he chattered on, like any normal boy, telling me about his friends in the Española Junior High and asking me questions just to make sure I was still with him.

I had totally lost track of time. I know now that Michael held me on that ledge for over two hours before more lights appeared in the canyon—David, with a doctor and two paramedics.

The ordeal they went through for the next several hours getting me off the cliff is another story. All I can say is that there were many acts of heroism from them all as they climbed the slippery rocks, splinting my leg and arm, strapping me into a litter, lowering me on ropes to the canyon floor. Michael acted as messenger, relaying instructions from one rescuer to another. All this in cold, wet darkness.

As groggy as I was, I still realized their terrible danger, and my prayer changed: *Please, God, don't let one of them die on this cliff in helping me.*

Because of a head injury I hadn't even known about, the doctor was not able to give me painkillers. My screams, every time I was accidentally jostled, had to be unnerving for the men, but they didn't give up. Even though they were cold and exhausted, they carried me as carefully as they could over the rough canyon floor and up the slopes to the pickup truck, then drove me over rocky jeep trails to the road where the ambulance waited. Because of the seriousness of my injuries, the doctors in Española couldn't treat me but sent me on to St. Vincent's Hospital in Santa Fe. At last, twelve hours after my fall, I went into surgery, where the doctors pieced my torn and broken body back together.

I awoke to find myself immobilized in heavy casts. Me, Ms. Independence, totally helpless and having to rely on others for everything—bedpans, baths, food, therapy. Dozens of flower arrangements and over a hundred cards arrived, soon filling my room. Friends and acquaintances flocked to see me, saying eagerly, "You've always been such a loner, Susan, holding us off. But at last we're going to get to do something for you!"

The God I met on that ledge was neither angry nor condemning. The God I met there was love. Love, flowing from an unseen Presence to give me strength; love, coming from David and the rescue team as they struggled to get me off the cliff; love from doctors, nurses, and old friends; and love from Michael, a child who sustained me during that lonely, painful night.

When that rock fell, so did the wall I'd built around myself to shut out that love. I will never be the same.

Irresistible Love

*For I am convinced that neither death, nor life,
nor angels, nor principalities, nor things present,
nor things to come, nor powers, nor height,
nor depth, nor any other created thing,
will be able to separate us from the love of God,
which is in Christ Jesus our Lord*

ROMANS 8:38–39 NASB

My Secret World

BY JANET LONG

It was another Sunday morning. Another day to be reminded that I had not truly worshiped God in months. Before I met Jonathan, the Lord was so important in my life—a close, personal Presence who loved me unfailingly from day to day. But now...

Across the breakfast table my husband, Harold, was finishing his methodical reading of the newspaper: first the front page, then the business news, then sports. *Orderly and predictable in everything,* I thought as I sipped my coffee—so different from Jonathan!

I winced at the comparison. When would I stop thinking about this man who had long since stopped thinking about me? *It's your own fault,* a mocking voice seemed to whisper. *You broke the rules. You played Jonathan's game and got hurt. Now here you are, a dissatisfied woman stuck in a barren marriage, with a secret you cannot share, a pain you cannot put away.*

Our young son, Jamie, was rolling his Hot Wheels car along the kitchen floor. "Mommy, are we going to church today?" he asked.

"Of course we are," I said automatically.

"Oh no!" he wailed. "I don't want to!" *Bam!* went the little red car into the wall.

"No tantrums, young man!" I said firmly. "You just go upstairs and start putting on your good clothes."

As I watched him trudge obediently up the stairs, I chided myself for being such a hypocrite. Sunday services were my greatest trial. During the week I could occupy my mind with my job and tasks at home—but at church I felt nothing but emptiness. It was like staring at God's back; He had tested me and I had failed.

"It's about time we got ready too," Harold said, glancing at his watch. I stood up and began clearing the table as Harold took away his own plate and neatly scraped the remnants of food into the garbage disposal. I knew all of his little habits so well. So methodical. So well-balanced. So sane. But never an unexpected compliment. Never a touch of his hand as we walked down the street. Never any more affection or understanding than he felt necessary.

"Pipe dreams," I could almost hear him saying as he did one night after a TV talk show about putting "romance" back into marriage. "All that moonlight and roses stuff. If a man works hard at his job and respects his wife and provides for his family, I don't know why that can't be enough."

I had been too discouraged to try to tell him that I needed more. And, strangely, in that same week, Jonathan joined the staff in the office where I worked part-time.

Almost from the beginning the intimacy was there. Here was someone who smiled easily, who listened, who made me feel important, intelligent, desirable. I wasn't a flirtatious woman, but I didn't know how terribly vulnerable, how hungry for attention I was. At first, when I realized that Jonathan was becoming too familiar, I refused to respond. We were both married. I knew what my marriage vows had promised. But Jonathan was determined to work his way into my life. He said he loved me. He insisted that I love him. Maybe it was because I was starved for simple human affection. But finally he succeeded in breaking down my resistance.

For a brief time we shared that secret world. But then, suddenly, the emotional cost—or the fear of discovery—became too great for Jonathan. Gradually I realized that our moments alone were becoming fewer. When we were together, what I began to hear was how marvelous his wife was and how he loved her.

Finally, in confusion and disbelief, I asked if he knew how much he was hurting me.

"I know," he said gently. "But if we continue I will only hurt you more."

Then Jonathan was gone, and half of me was missing.

My mourning was as severe as if he had died. There was no one with whom I could share this secret sorrow. I was afraid to trust a friend, ashamed to tell my minister, and there was no money for a counselor. There might have been prayer, but I felt too miserable and too filled with remorse to try to talk to God.

Alone I struggled with the numbness I felt toward my marriage, with the despair of knowing that for me there was nothing more than the emotionally barren life I lived with my husband. Depression set in. Weeks of it.

The sharpness of my pain had subsided, but now I couldn't even cry. What I felt now, this deadness inside, was the worst of all....

It was a short drive to church and we arrived just as the entry hymn began. Our two children—Susie and Jamie—were between Harold and me. Jamie was already restless, scuffing the pew in front and jiggling the hymnal just enough to make reading the words impossible. I participated in the singing and the prayers, but none of it touched me. I just felt empty inside.

But then something unusual happened. One of the members of the choir stepped to the pulpit to make an announcement. A sudden hush fell over the congregation.

"This morning's hymn," he said, "was composed by a grieving father after the death of his child. Today the choir dedicates it to any members of this congregation experiencing deep need."

Softly the notes of the organ began, and then with beautiful clarity from the tenor soloist came these words:

Sometimes the load is heavy

And sometimes the road is long....

Like an illness borne too long, the abscess of pain with which I had struggled opened. Tears sprang to my eyes, quietly washing down my cheeks. I heard only the music, gentle and soothing, touched with deep but restrained feeling. It was not until the end that I heard the words again, and they were, "Thy will be done."

I had not lost a son. The music of someone whose pain had been far greater than my own had sent the message that hope and faith can triumph over sorrow. I knew that that message was specifically for me.

After the song was over, the minister moved to the pulpit to deliver the sermon, and again I had the conviction that there would be something in it especially for me.

Clearing his throat, our minister began:

Today's text is from John, chapter twenty-one. "After breakfast, Jesus said to Simon Peter, 'Simon, son of John, do you love Me more than all else?' 'Yes, Lord,' he answered, 'You know that I love You.' 'Then feed My lambs,' He said. A second time He asked, 'Simon, son of John, do you love Me?' 'Yes, Lord, You know I love You.' 'Then tend My sheep.' A third time He said, 'Simon, son of John, do you love Me?'

"Peter was hurt that He asked him a third time, 'Do you love Me?' 'Lord,' he said, 'You know everything; You know I love You.' Jesus said, 'Feed My sheep.' "

Why had I never noticed before, I asked myself incredulously, that Peter had denied Christ three times after his arrest and that

Christ's response had been to give him three opportunities to profess his love?

In this marvelous passage, Peter, the sinner, was forgiven, and in the forgiving, full faith and trust in him was restored. Now, when I had messed up my life and could not even pray, God loved me enough to reach out on this quiet Sunday and let me know it. I felt illuminated with Christ's love and forgiveness, as though the sun were shining right into my heart, warming it and bringing it once again to life.

Feed My sheep, I repeated to myself in wonder. That was the way Jesus accepted Peter's love: by giving him a ministry of love to others. I glanced over at Harold's calm face, seeing suddenly all the good qualities—strength, patience, dependability.

Could I rebuild my marriage and my life? In a surge of confidence, I felt I could.

Through the hopeful song of someone who had lost his child, God had shown me that no sorrow or trouble was too great for His love to heal. He had spoken to me again through the Scripture, assuring me of His unlimited willingness to forgive. What more certainty did I need?

When I walked out of the church building with my family, I knew I was walking into a new life. Although this was just the beginning and there was perhaps a long way to go, I felt at peace with myself and my husband. Christ had shown me the way to follow Him: "Feed My sheep."

Love Is...

Love is patient, love is kind....
It does not dishonor others,
it is not self-seeking....
It always protects, always trusts,
always hopes, always perseveres.
Love never fails....
Now these three remain: faith, hope and love.
But the greatest of these is love.

1 CORINTHIANS 13:4–5, 7–8, 13 NIV

It Could Happen to You

BY CATHERINE CLARK

O ur new car was like a dream come true. My husband and I had planned on it for so long. Like two kids with a Christmas toy, we inspected every detail—trying out the windshield wipers, tuning in the radio, opening the glove compartment.

The dream car arrived while my sister and her family were spending a few days of their vacation with us. Although expecting my second baby and warned to keep my activities to a minimum, I decided, impulsively, to go with my sister to her Texas home. The following weekend, Clark (everyone calls him by our last name) was to drive down and pick me up in our new car.

While packing, I was suddenly haunted by an inexplicable regret of my decision, but brushed it aside as a silly notion. *Of course I want to go and see everyone,* I argued with myself. *In a few months I won't be able to move around at all.*

I'll never forget how my husband looked when we drove away as he turned and waved goodbye.

During the five wonderful years of our marriage, we had a pet habit of silently forming the words, "I love you," with our lips. It was a little secret game we played over the heads of our friends at parties or wherever we might be. The one who said it first won the game for that time.

Now as Clark turned and waved, he beat me at our game.

My week's visit at my sister's home was darkened by a strange fear I could not explain. I was glad when the weekend arrived and I looked forward to seeing my husband.

On Friday night, we sat on my sister's front lawn, waiting. Hours passed. I grew nervously impatient and my eyes were glued to the direction I knew our car would approach—but it never came. At midnight, feeling some business must have detained him, we all went to bed. I stretched out fully dressed and finally fell asleep.

The piercing ring of the telephone woke me at 5 a.m.

During the moments that followed tears and words were mixed together; facts jumbled. Then we threw suitcases into my sister's car, and to the steady drone of wheels I tried to piece the story together.

A head-on collision at early dusk. Two killed. Four seriously injured. Some of these might not live—one not more than two hours at the most. And that one was my husband!

In just two small hours—or even less—all of the fun and laughter, all of our wonderful crazy dreams, the little game we played—all of it would be gone forever.

I closed my eyes and prayed. My small son sat in my lap, the very image of his dad. With his fat little finger he solemnly wiped at my tears as they slid down my cheeks and asked, "Why Mommy cry?"

The doctors did not want me to see my husband, but they could not stop me. They warned me about my pregnancy, but I ignored them and entered Clark's room.

I looked at him once, then kept staring at his ring. It was the only way I could recognize him, he was so smashed up. Then I reached out to him, but the nurse held me back.

"You mustn't touch him," she said. "The pain will be too much."

I sank slowly into the chair, suddenly realizing that there had been others in the accident. Where were they? How badly were they hurt? Did they look like this? And what about the driver of the other car?

Later I learned about him. My husband and friends had been at a business conference, and returning home in the evening twilight hour they rounded a curve in the highway and saw a car bearing down, on the wrong side of the road.

A man had driven too far. A good man but a tired one. He had fallen asleep at the wheel.

I wanted to hate him. I wanted to rush to him and demand: "Do you know what you've done to us—to all of us? Do you know you've killed two people? One was someone dear to me; one was someone dear to you. Do you realize you've disfigured two people in a terrible way? Why didn't you stop when you knew you were so tired?"

Yet something kept reminding me of my own life: the times we had hurried, the times we were tired on the road when, by the grace of God, we escaped being the guilty one. We had always been lucky. None of us were bad people, just thoughtless people—sure of our driving, sure of our cars, sure of everything... until we were struck down.

Sitting in my husband's room, I thought of all that. Suddenly Clark stretched out his hand. Carefully, I placed mine in it and his fingers curled lovingly and tenderly about mine as though, through some miraculous power, he knew I was there. There was no need to form the words of my prayer. Clark did rally and fought desperately to live.

The painful days ebbed away. My mother-in-law and I had taken a room in the nearby home of a minister and his wife. They were wonderful people, and though we were of different faiths, I knew he was praying for my husband.

One afternoon Clark suddenly took a turn for the worse. It was evident that he was dying. His mother and I faced each other across his bed. I asked her if she wanted me to get a minister and she said yes.

I hurried down the street to the minister we knew and, in silence, the two of us ran back to the hospital. Quietly he took my husband's hand and knelt beside his bed.

Something then happened in that small hospital room which is beyond understanding. Although the door was closed, it seemed suddenly that light was coming through it. The brightness pierced my closed eyes so strongly that I opened them and looked around, sensing the nearness of someone else in the room. I stepped to Clark and took his hand. It was growing warmer.

The door burst open and the doctor rushed in. Even as he worked over my husband, he said he had a fighting chance again. But I felt I had already been told that....

We are home now and my husband is well. Once again my husband and I can sit in crowded rooms and play our secret game of "I love you."

Count the Ways

How do I love thee? Let me count the ways.
I love thee to the depth and breadth and height
My soul can reach, when feeling out of sight...
I love thee with the breath,
Smiles, tears, of all my life!

ELIZABETH BARRETT BROWNING

Ricky Loves Cindy

BY RICKY WARD

I started courting Cindy when we were in our teens. I still remember the day we scrambled into a ravine near her father's farm in Trenton, Florida, and carved our names and a crude heart into an old bridge. Cindy was the only girl I ever really noticed. Her brown hair bounced when she walked down the hall at our high school, and her smile always brightened my day. But if I caught anyone else noticing Cindy—man, watch out! I had a jealous streak a mile wide. Truth is, it nearly broke us up.

The summer after Cindy and I started dating, her dad invited me to work on his farm. I said yes before he could finish asking. I saw Cindy every day of summer vacation, since she worked in the fields with about a half dozen of us guys. It was hot, dirty work and we all wore shorts, including Cindy. That kind of bothered me.

One day Cindy and I were walking back to the house after a long afternoon of picking. My blood was simmering, and not just because of the heartless Florida heat. Finally I blurted it out: "I saw you flirting with that guy out in the field today, Cindy!"

Cindy stopped and took a deep breath. "Ricky Ward, I was not flirting with anybody," she said evenly. "You can't keep on being so jealous like this!"

I turned away, ashamed. I didn't want to make a fool of myself but I just couldn't shake this crazy feeling that came over me every time I saw Cindy talking to another guy. Fact was, I had no reason whatsoever not to trust Cindy. I knew she was my girl. She came from good people, a fine, churchgoing family that had practically taken me in. Her father and I hit it off so well that I began calling him Pa. My family was not churchgoing then, so I started going with Cindy's. Soon I found a faith of my own, and Pa helped me study the Bible to learn more about God.

But I didn't use my new faith much that summer toiling in Pa's fields. I hated it if Cindy paid attention to anyone but me, and we had several blowups over my jealousy. Each ended with me begging for forgiveness and promising to change.

But if working in the fields with Cindy gave me fits, returning to school that fall pushed me over the edge. Cindy had only to say hi to another boy and I'd begin to fume. Man, it felt as if my blood were on fire!

One evening when I was over at Cindy's for dinner, Pa called me out to the backyard for a talk. "Son," he said, "I can see you think the world of Cindy, and she's pretty high on you too. I know you two are getting serious about marriage. But, son, you've got to do something about that jealous temper of yours."

As we talked, I found myself studying the ground. "Now look here," Pa said, "I want you to get out the Scriptures and read the thirteenth chapter of 1 Corinthians, especially verse four. Study it good, and keep reminding yourself of it whenever these jealous spells come on you. Remember, you can trust Cindy."

"Yes, sir," I said as we headed back inside. Later I looked up the verse: "Love is patient and kind; love is not jealous...." *Try*, I thought. *Try to control it. For Cindy and Pa.*

Then one night I swung by Cindy's house. I'd just bought a new pickup truck with my after-school earnings and we were going to celebrate with a pizza. I sauntered up the walk, breathing in the sharp smell of woodsmoke from the chimney. Cindy came out looking as pretty as I'd ever seen her. She wore the pink knit dress that I liked so much and her hair shone under the porch light. "Let's go!" she sang out.

But later, as we held hands in a back booth of the pizzeria, some fellows from the football team burst in. One gave Cindy a big smile and what I took to be an overly friendly hello. I pulled Cindy out of the booth. "Let's go," I muttered as we headed outside.

All the way home I ranted and raved while Cindy stared out the window. "It's because I love you so much that I feel this way!" I kept insisting. It was what I always said.

She was having none of it. As we walked up to the front porch, Cindy fought back sobs. I was scared. I'd never seen her this upset. "Ricky," she said, barely able to get the words out, "I can't take it anymore. I can't marry you if you're like this." With that, she dashed inside, the door banging shut behind her.

It was a long trip back to my house—twenty miles of taking a good hard look at myself and where my jealous streak had taken me. "Lord, I don't want to lose Cindy," I cried, banging the steering wheel. "I love her!" The verse from 1 Corinthians came back to me: love is not jealous. I'd been telling myself that love was the reason I was so crazy-jealous. But the Bible says that love and jealousy can't coexist. I couldn't love Cindy and be jealous at the same time. My jealousy was hurting the woman I loved.

As soon as I got home I pulled out my Bible and turned to 1 Corinthians. *Dear God*, I prayed, *take away my jealous heart. Help me to learn to trust You and those who love me. I've tried to do it myself, and I can't. Amen.*

When I awoke the next morning I felt as if a terrible weight had been lifted from me. At school I spotted Cindy by her locker. She wasn't wearing my prized blue and gold Future Farmers of America jacket, but who could blame her? "I'm sorry," I said. I didn't make any excuses.

Just then the boy from the night before strolled by and let out a cheery "Hello, Cindy!" She flinched, dreading my reaction. But all I did was smile and look her right in the eye. "Honey," I said, "things are going to get a lot better. You'll see."

With the Lord's help, they sure did. Cindy and I were married the spring we graduated from high school. Whenever I felt the old twinge coming back, I just recited my verse. Love, I understand now, is never jealous. It is a pure, unconditional gift from God.

Eventually Cindy and I moved up to Georgia and started a family. We still get down to Florida to visit Pa and the rest of Cindy's family, though. We were there one February years later. On a bright, crisp morning Cindy and I took a walk and climbed down a ravine near the farm. There it was, barely visible, two names and a heart scratched into an old bridge: RICKY LOVES CINDY, OCTOBER 3, 1973.

Cindy's eyes glistened as I pulled her close and whispered my Valentine's Day postscript: "Still does!"

The Power of Love

*I love you for putting your hand into my
heaped-up heart and passing over all the foolish,
weak things that you can't help dimly seeing there,
and for drawing out into the light all the beautiful
belongings that no one else had looked
quite far enough to find.*

ROY CROFT

How to Love the Unloving

BY BETHANNE WALKER

I t became a sore point in my life, nagging at me daily. Never had I known a person who openly disliked me. And to make matters worse, this woman was my father's new wife.

They married a short time after Mother's death. My husband and I felt it was too soon, but Dad convinced us he was in love. So, with high expectations, we made a special effort to include her in our family.

Dad's life and home had been built on the open-arms policy, but all that soon changed. We were no longer welcome to drop by the small house. Even our phone calls were intercepted by an impatient "What do you want with him?"

As the months went by, I continued to make friendly overtures. After all, I had always tried to be a decent person. Why should someone simply not like me? But when we met in town, my stepmother would ignore my efforts at conversation, or even pretend she didn't see me.

Christmas arrived, and thinking it was a good time to set things right, I took a homemade mincemeat pie to my father and stepmother. I felt a little better after the short visit. Her cool reception had been warmed somewhat by Dad's enthusiastic thanks. But before I could get off the porch, I heard her say, "No, I don't like mincemeat pie! And you probably don't either. You just won't tell her."

For the first time in my life I felt like throwing a pie in someone's face. But I knew anger wouldn't help—nor my tears of frustration. Either because of her jealousy or plain unwillingness to share this man, we were being shoved out.

It hurt even more to watch my children. The two-year-old began to take her baby-sitting couple for her grandparents. Our young son begged to see his "Papa," who had lavished affection on him since birth. Our teenage daughter looked the other way when we passed their house, aching about something that I couldn't change—or even explain.

One morning I sat down as usual for devotions. The Bible verse for the day read, "For if ye love them which love you, what thank have ye? for sinners also love those that love them" (Luke 6:32 KJV). I bristled with indignation. Some people you just can't love! I insisted. But I knew, as God's child, that loving those who loved me was nothing special. That was easy. But to love someone who apparently hated me—that would be God's way.

How can I? I wondered. I glanced over more of the Scripture passage in front of me (Luke 6:27–32)—and the guidelines were right there!

1. "Love your enemies...." I began to try to look at my stepmother through God's eyes and focus on good qualities. *She treasures my dad,* I told myself. *She takes excellent care of*

Mother's cat. She's a spotless housekeeper, and she nurses her invalid mother.

2. "Do good to them which hate you...." Since I couldn't approach my stepmother in person, I started sending a sunny card or tiny gift from time to time, signing myself "Someone who cares." I hoped this might lift her on a bad day.

3. "Pray for them which despitefully use you." This was tough! But it got easier each day. I prayed out loud, so I could hear my own voice asking God to bless her, to love her through me.

Today, from my practical earthly viewpoint, I can see no change in the situation. But by following these three steps, I am sometimes lifted to a higher view where I do see a gradual change—not in my stepmother, perhaps, but in me. I am learning a different kind of love, loving without expecting something in return. It's difficult to put into action and slow to grow. But staggering in its practical and spiritual potential.

Eyes of Love

God looks at the world through the eyes of love. If we, therefore, as human beings made in the image of God also want to see reality...as it truly is, then we too must learn to look at what we see with love.

ROBERTA BONDI

Vigil for a Little Boy

BY SALLY JOHN

W hen our little boy Travis fell out of a third-story window, it was all over the news. But there was even more to the story than what most people probably read or heard about on TV.

Ironically, the weeks preceding the accident were the best we'd had as a family in all the years of my husband Tommy's major-league career. The baseball strike was on, and as difficult as it was for the players, those weeks had given us precious time together for picnics and fun with our three children—Tami, seven; young Tommy, four; and Travis, two-and-a-half (not to mention their soon-to-be-born baby brother, whom I was then carrying).

The strike was over in early August—and on the thirteenth, with Tommy on the road again, I accepted an invitation to visit our dear friends Chuck and Carol Schaefer and their three children at the Jersey Shore. I come from Indiana and have never been crazy about the ocean, so all the way there in the car I warned the children: "Remember, the ocean can be dangerous. The waves can pull you out—Travis, are you listening?"

Travis was a child whom I thought of as an accident-waiting-to-happen. If you told him, "Don't touch that," he'd touch it. I could see the gleam in his eyes; he was ready to race into that ocean.

"Travis," I said firmly, "you've got to watch out for sharks. Do you know what a shark is? It's a big fish that bites your toes off." That seemed to impress him.

We arrived at the Schaefers' rented house, which was large and beautiful. My sister Judy and four of her five children had been invited too. After an afternoon on the beach, we returned to the house to dress for an evening on the boardwalk.

I had just finished dressing. The boys were playing quietly in one of the bedrooms; the house hummed with low-key, late-afternoon activity. And then, in an instant, the peace was shattered. "Mommy, Mommy!" my daughter Tami screamed. "Travis just fell out of the window!"

In an instant I was down the stairs and into the yard. *I hope he didn't bump his mouth*, I thought, *or chip a tooth*. It was only when I rounded the corner of the house that the reality of what had happened hit me. Travis's little body lay on the concrete driveway, completely still.

I looked up three stories to the window where the other children stared down in stunned disbelief. I rushed forward and picked up Travis, hugging him to me. He was limp in my arms. Blood trickled from one ear, his skin was blue, he wasn't breathing. His head hung at a grotesque angle. *He's broken his neck!* I thought. *This can't be happening.*

"My baby's dead!" I screamed aloud.

Through Travis's parted lips I could see the underside of his tongue that had slipped backward into his throat. I tried to reach in with my fingers, but his jaw was locked. Moving him onto the grass, I groped for a stick, for anything to pry his mouth open. There was nothing. *Help me, God!*

The nail-polish bottle! It was still clutched in my hand. I had been about to put it in my makeup kit when Tami first screamed. Forcing the rounded top into his mouth, I pried his teeth apart and unfolded his tongue. With a rattling gasp, Travis started to breathe.

The police and the neighbors were there almost immediately. Travis and I were bundled into the backseat of a squad car, and we were rushed to Point Pleasant Hospital. While Judy and Carol filled out the necessary forms, I frantically telephoned Tommy in Detroit, where the Yankees were playing the Tigers that night. Finally, Tommy came on the line. How does a wife tell her husband that his son may be dying?

"Tommy," I screamed. "Travis fell from a window! I think he's broken his neck. I'm...not sure,"

"What? What?" he shouted from a thousand miles away.

"Tommy, just hurry," I cried into the phone. "Please, just get here!" I needed him by my side desperately.

I hung up the phone and stood there with Carol and Judy and cried as I'd never cried before. A nurse came and put her arms around me and asked if I'd like to go to the chapel. Mutely I nodded.

In the chapel, I dropped to the floor in despair. In a fit of grief and anger, I cried out, "Lord, this can't have happened—not to Travis! I know things happen for a reason, Lord, but there can't be any good in this. I'll do anything, but don't take Travis!"

I stormed, I bargained, I begged. I could not, I would not live without my Travis. I didn't want to be tested by God! I just wanted my baby alive and well.

In that little chapel, my friend Carol, my sister Judy, and I walked and prayed; we kicked the walls and cried, then prayed again. I tried to say the words, "Our Father, who art in Heaven... Thy will be done." But my heart cried, *No, Father, not Your will but mine be done! Let my little son live—please!*

I called the pastor of our former church, Gene Ongna, in California. His reassurances were what I needed to hear at that moment. He said he would call the church prayer chain, and added, "Sally, remember we all love you."

We went back to the hospital ward to wait. Two nurses appeared to tell us that Travis miraculously had suffered no broken bones. I couldn't believe that his neck really wasn't broken. But I was told there was a slight skull fracture and signs of hemorrhaging; the doctors wanted to do a cranial exploratory. They asked me to sign a consent form for the operation.

"I can't just sign my child's life away," I said. "I've got to talk to somebody." I was told there was no time for a call. If I did not sign now, my son might die.

I signed, and the waiting began. One and a half hours dragged by. It seemed like fifteen years.

At 9:10 p.m. a doctor came out and told us that Travis had made it through surgery. They had relieved the pressure on his brain. But he was still unconscious and it was too early to tell if there was permanent brain damage.

They let me see him. It was terrible: his little head was shaved, wires and tubes were coming out of him everywhere, and there were ice bags all around his head. His arms and legs were moving, but I was told these were only reflex actions. But thank God he wasn't paralyzed. I touched his hand and wept.

Tommy finally arrived at 1:00 a.m. A friend who had played golf with him earlier in the day had offered the use of his private plane. He arrived fully prepared to be told Travis was dead. Now together we thanked God that at least our son was alive.

Then Tommy received a call from a friend in California, Dr. Stu Siegel, who had heard the news on his car radio. Stu wanted to know if there was anything he could do.

"Where can Travis get the best treatment?" Tommy asked.

"Call Dr. Fred Epstein at the New York University Medical Center," Stu replied. "He's the best pediatric neurosurgeon in the entire country. And they've got all the latest equipment at the Center."

After a sleepless night, we placed a call to Dr. Epstein. He conferred on the phone with the surgeons at Point Pleasant and then recommended that Travis be flown immediately to New York. The surgeons who had operated on Travis disagreed; they said that Travis might not survive the helicopter flight.

It was an agonizing decision for Tommy and me. We prayed earnestly, and then followed our instinct that Dr. Epstein was right. Having made up our minds, we placed Travis in God's hands.

We arrived at the NYU Medical Center at 10:30 a.m. and were met by Dr. Epstein and a team of doctors, and then they were wheeling our little boy down the hallway away from us. We stood there, helpless to do anything for Travis except pray.

After another seemingly endless wait, Dr. Epstein emerged. "Travis is in serious condition," he said. "But we don't see any sign of irreversible brain damage. We're going to do some tests to make sure—but we think he's going to be okay." Tommy and I fell into each other's arms in joyous relief. I think it was the most important news that either of us has ever heard.

But Travis remained in a coma. Days and nights went by. Hour after hour we hovered by his bedside waiting for some sign that would indicate he was waking up. There was none.

As one day slipped into another and Travis remained in his trancelike sleep, Tommy reluctantly returned to the Yankees. Tommy has the gift of being able to concentrate under pressure, and it was a relief for him to release his tension by playing ball after the long, frustrating hours at the hospital. Reporters dogged him, plying him with questions. But even the reporters asked,

"What can we do?" And Tommy would reply, "You can pray, and ask everyone else to pray too." And they did.

When Tommy wasn't playing, he was with me at Travis's bedside. We'd sit there—Tommy and Carol and I—gently stroking Travis's arms, his hair, his cheek. And we'd talk to him: "Travis, wake up, honey! Tami misses you, Little Tommy misses you. We all love you—please open your eyes. Travis, come back!"

Gradually, as the days passed, I became more and more aware of the magnitude of the response outside the hospital. From the first day of Travis's accident, Tommy and I were unprepared for the outpouring of concern. People we hadn't heard from in years—and others whom we didn't know at all—called and wrote to say they were praying for us. Stacks and stacks of letters began to arrive from all over the country and from as far away as Guam—thousands of them. Some of the letters were addressed simply to "Travis John, New York City." But we got them all. And we felt them all.

There were enough flowers to stock a florist shop. Since flowers are forbidden in intensive care, Tommy and I thought we should share them with others. We had a grand time bringing flowers and even toys to other sick children in the hospital, some of whom had not even one get-well card. We told the children that they were from their friend Travis.

One day, after Travis had been in his coma for over a week, Terence Cardinal Cooke, Archbishop of New York, visited us.

We are not Roman Catholics, but we were deeply touched by this man of God. He told us, "Sally and Tommy, it's clear you have so much love in your hearts for your baby. And your love, and the love of thousands of people from all over the country, is being transmitted through you to Travis. Keep pouring that love out to that baby, because love heals." Then the Cardinal prayed with us.

And there were others who prayed—the parents of other sick children. They told us that they were beseeching God to save our child's life, sometimes while their own children were dying.

As far as being in the "cold" city, well, New Yorkers were anything but cold. I remember in particular a big Irish cop named Mike, whose little boy Jerry was also very ill. One day I saw him holding Jerry on his lap. "Oh, Mike," I said, "how I long for the day when I can hold Travis on my lap again."

"Look, I know Travis is going to be okay," he replied. "Because with all those people praying for him, heaven will never be at rest if he isn't all right."

I could almost see heaven in chaos over Travis. It brought a smile to my face. Mike's faith was infectious.

We continued our vigil at Travis's bedside, watching, waiting, praying for a sign. His arms and legs still moved reflexively, but what we longed to see was any movement that seemed deliberate, that indicated he knew what he was doing.

And then, on the sixteenth day, came the moment I will never forget. As I sat gazing at my silent son, he suddenly lifted his tiny hand and rubbed his eye! It was the miracle we had been praying for! We called out excitedly to Dr. Epstein, who was with a child in the next cubicle.

We had been told that Travis would not wake up dramatically all at once, and Dr. Epstein warned us that Travis might not move again for days, or even months. But Travis had other ideas. Within a few days his eyes were open. But his throat was too sore from the tubes for him to be able to speak yet.

Finally, on the twenty-second day, his lips parted, and I leaned close to his small face. What would his first words be? Would they be tender endearments for his mother? I held my breath as he croaked out his first precious sentiments: "I'm hungwy!" he said.

But a short time later he did whisper the words I'd been longing to hear all through those dark days and nights. "I wuv you, Mommy," he said, reaching up to put his arms around my neck.

A year later, Travis was fully recovered and just as mischievous as ever. His beautiful blond curls had grown back, and I reluctantly faced the prospect of having his hair cut.

As terrible as our ordeal was, Tommy and I learned and grew from it. We discovered in a deep, personal way what it cost God to give up His Son to suffering and death for you and me. We couldn't have offered Travis up like that, and yet God did. How much He must love the world to have done that.

And we discovered something else from doctors and nurses and hospital personnel who worked around the clock, from people like you, people from all walks of life, all ages and all faiths, who showered us with letters and calls and prayers: Tommy and I discovered how much we need one another.

All of us will have to face heartbreaking grief or a life-and-death crisis sooner or later, and when this happens, don't hug your grief to your heart. Don't try to go it alone. Reach out to those around you—to family, friends, your church. Share your sorrow and your need, if it's only to say "pray for me" or "let me know you're standing by." Don't be afraid to ask for help, for there are reservoirs of strength everywhere, in the prayers of friends, the touch of a loving hand, a sympathetic glance. And then, whatever happens—because in spite of all our love and prayers, we might have lost Travis—don't shut yourself off. Reach out. Reach out to receive the boundless love of God.

In our affliction, thousands of you reached out to us. Though we may never meet personally, we want you to know that without your caring, Tommy and I wouldn't have made it. And we think that faith played a big part in our little boy's recovery.

Reach Out

Love makes burdens lighter,
because you divide them.
It makes joys more intense,
because you share them.
It makes you stronger,
so that you can reach out
and become involved with life
in ways you dared not risk alone.

UNKNOWN

Trouble at the Indy 500

BY BONNI LIBHART

L ike a malevolent red demon, the Indy 500 pace car came streaking straight toward me, my husband, Tony, and fifty fellow journalists crowded on a flimsy press stand in the pit area of the Indianapolis Motor Speedway.

"Hey, the pace car's lost control!"

"They're going too fast."

"It's going to hit..."

In seconds, the open convertible carrying former astronaut John Glenn and three other race officials careened off the track, skidded over the apron, and now—before any of us could do more than register the horror of the inevitable crash—it slammed through a safety fence and into our bleachers. Around me, splintered two-by-fours from the handrail of the temporary stand rained down. Human figures bounced and ricocheted from the steps like drops of water on a hot grill, and I was somersaulted into the air. I landed on the pace car's hood and slipped to the ground.

O Lord, is this death?

In shock, moving in slow motion, I automatically began to grope for our belongings...but where was Tony? I raised my head and saw men pulling my husband from the steaming hood of the pace car, his white jeans and shirt spattered with blood.

Still dazed, I crawled to Tony's side. He was unconscious. But my own mind was now fully awake, and though my body was bruised, it was my swarming thoughts that hurt and stung. *O God, help me. I brought Tony here to keep him quiet—to forward my career. Did I bring him here to die?*

On that Saturday in May 1971, I was one of the first two women reporters ever allowed in the servicing pits and garage areas during the running of the annual 500-mile car race in Indianapolis. At the time, I worked as hostess-producer of my own daily television interview program in Jonesboro, Arkansas. When the station's sports director found he couldn't cover the internationally famous competition, he gave me the choice assignment. And in order to placate my husband, who resented my frequent trips away from our home and three children, I decided to use him as the photographer on the story. A design engineer professionally, Tony was also a first-rate hand with a camera—and I knew that he'd dreamed of going to the "500" since boyhood.

Tony and I had successfully covered other news events for KAIT-TV as a reporter-photographer team. But in recent years our marriage partnership had developed all the marks of failure. Oh, not in the material sense. We both earned good money, and I saw to it that we lived to the limit of our two incomes. We had a brand-new two-story Tudor house, a gold color 280-S Mercedes, and expensive wardrobes, including my white mink coat. We also had sarcasm, nagging, accusations, and self-justification.

"You ought to spend more time with the kids, Bonni."

"And you ought to help me more around the house."

"Well, I can't be a mother—that's your job."

"In case you've forgotten, my job brings in the most money."

Sniping and bickering, then bitterness and even hatred. Unbelievably, we had somehow come to the most vicious words of all: I wish you were dead.

Mixed with the monstrous roar of the cars on the racetrack, the sounds of disaster filled my ears—cries for help, the keen wail of the ambulance sirens, the *whop-whop* of the rescue helicopters overhead. Altogether, twenty-four people were tumbled on the infield grass with broken arms or legs, internal injuries, bleeding wounds. Kneeling beside my husband, I heard my own voice screaming and pleading for a doctor. Minutes crawled by at a snail's pace until an ambulance was able to inch its way backward through the crowd and take Tony to the track's hospital, which turned out to be little more than a first-aid station.

At last a nurse and doctor began attending to Tony, and I allowed myself to be taken to another area for treatment. Apart from bruises and a slight concussion, I had not been injured, and as I was being checked, I was relieved to hear that Tony had been moved to Methodist Hospital in downtown Indianapolis. But when I went back outside the tent, I saw that he was still lying on an army cot in a group of other injured newsmen. They had taken someone else.

Trembling, I stretched out on the grass alongside Tony's pallet. The right side of his face, neck, and chest were turning an angry purple, and his cheek was an inch lower than normal. Most terrifying of all, both his eyes were swollen shut. Nausea began to rise in my throat. Tony was alive. Was he going to be blind?

So many times at home, I'd "lose" our car in a crowded parking lot. Tony always seemed to know where to find it. "You look, but you don't see," he'd tell me.

Tony was a reserved person, quiet and observant. I was the glad-hander and chatterbox. After all, an introvert doesn't get to be the hostess of a television talk show. Around Jonesboro, Tony was known as Mr. Bonni Libhart. Naturally, that bugged him. And deep down, he surely sensed that my respect for him was tempered by the fact that my salary was bigger than his—and that I compared him unfavorably to the flashier and more aggressive men I worked with.

I'd grown up in the country, hardscrabble poor, in a house with no electricity and no indoor bathroom. With my background of rural poverty, I had a strong incentive to achieve. I was proud of my success and the local celebrity it brought. I used my fat paycheck to indulge my passion for "nice" things—and if we didn't have cash available for something I wanted, my buying philosophy was "charge ahead."

Blind spending, blind ambition, blind to my love for Tony. Oh, God, why couldn't I see it before?

Three hours had passed since Tony's head had smashed against the windshield of the pace car. Now, abruptly, he began to vomit blood. The doctor who had examined him earlier dashed over and began to snap orders. "I thought this man had been taken to the hospital hours ago. Put him on intravenous and get him into a chopper right now."

The helicopter arrived and, with it, another setback. There would only be room aboard for Tony's stretcher, the attendant, and the pilot. I would have to find the hospital by myself. Standing among strangers, I watched the weird-looking, raucous machine lift Tony away into the sky. *I'm completely alone*, I thought.

But of course I wasn't.

With God's help, I managed to find our car—after half an hour—among the thousands in the speedway's parking bays. A sympathetic policeman gave me directions to the hospital. Though cars were traveling sixteen abreast on the highway, traffic was moving freely on the route I needed to take. More quickly than I had imagined possible, I was in the hospital's emergency ward listening to Tony's medical report. When his condition stabilized he would require surgery for a broken neck and jaw injuries, but his eyes had not been damaged.

I made a few telephone calls to reassure our family, then went to a small waiting room and collapsed in a chair. Picking up a magazine, I tried to read, but the printed words dissolved into prayer-thoughts. *Dear God, he's such a good man. The right man for me. Why do our jobs set us against each other? We're always competing, arguing about everything from how to raise the children to whose turn it is to take out the garbage. Why can't we pull together?*

For the first time that day, I cried. Tears coursed down my cheeks, and my false eyelashes came loose. Clumsily, I peeled them off and held them in my hand—two limp black strips that were supposed to create a glamorous illusion. What a fitting symbol for me! So much of my life was based on superficial values, so much of my energy diverted to making things look good on the outside. That's what blinded me to my love for Tony.

I was little more than a "committee Christian," unused to soul-baring prayer, but at that moment I fell to my knees. *Forgive me, God. Let Tony forgive me, too. Heal him, Lord, and help me heal myself and our marriage.*

Tony was not fully conscious until the following morning. I stood at his bedside, looking into his eyes.

"Tony, will you forgive me? I love you." My voice shook on the first few words but gained strength. "I want to try to start over—with God and you and the kids and my job all in the right order. Will you let me try...can we try?"

He was silent for several heartbeats, gazing at me steadily. "Yes, I'll try," he said quietly. "I know I can do more at home. I know I should open up to you more. Let's ask God to help us."

Tony's body mended slowly; the healing of our marriage took longer still.

But step by step, we worked out an agenda to break the pattern of opposition in our lives. We worshiped together at home and at church. We agreed to keep business trips and hours to a reasonable limit in order to devote as much time as possible to our family. We consulted each other about family activities and discipline for the children. When it came to family duties and responsibilities, we tried to swallow the word "your" and say the word "our."

In addition, I turned money matters over to Tony. He was clearly much better at financial management than I. The hidden benefit here was the new respect I gained for Tony's wisdom and ability.

Since the day the Indy 500 Pace car struck us, I've recognized that God used the shock of a sudden, life-threatening accident to help us revive and revitalize a dying marriage.

What's more, I've found a prayer to claim as my own (Psalm 119:37 RSV): "Turn my eyes from looking at vanities; and give me life in thy ways."

The Way of Love

The way is long—let us go together.
The way is difficult—let us help each other.
The way is joyful—let us share it.
The way is ours alone—let us go in love.

UNKNOWN

The Great Vacation Experiment

BY TOM ANDERSON

I made the vow to myself on the drive down to the beach cottage we'd rented for our vacation on the Jersey Shore. For two weeks I would try to be the loving husband and father Evelyn had always wanted me to be. Totally loving. No ifs, ands, or buts about it.

The idea for this drastic experiment had come to me as I listened to the voice of a Christian marriage counselor on the car's CD player. "You husbands must be careful of your wives, being thoughtful of their needs," the voice said, quoting 1 Peter 3:17 (TLB). I knew that I had often been a selfish kind of husband, probably much too self-centered, but as a partner in the Wall Street investment firm of Bear Stearns, I worked hard. So, after all, I deserved a bit of coddling.

"Love is an act of will. A person can choose to love," said the voice on the tape. Ashamedly, I had to admit that with Evelyn I often failed to choose love. In petty ways, really. Chiding her for her tardiness; insisting on the TV channel I wanted to watch; in my attitude that yesterday's news is worthless, throwing out day-old newspapers that I knew Evelyn still wanted to read. Well, for two weeks all that would change.

And it did. Right from the moment I kissed Evelyn at the door and said, "Honey, that new yellow sweater looks great on you."

"Oh, Tom, you noticed," she said, obviously surprised and pleased. Maybe a little perplexed.

After the long drive down, I wanted to sit and read. Evelyn suggested a walk on the beach. I started to refuse, but then I thought, *Evelyn's been alone here with the kids all week and now she wants to be alone with me.* We walked on the beach, while the kids flew their kites.

So it went. Two weeks of not calling the office; a visit to the shell museum, though I usually hate museums (and I enjoyed it); holding my tongue while Evelyn's getting ready made us late for a dinner date with friends. Relaxed and happy, that's how the whole vacation passed, so much so that I made a new vow to keep on remembering 1 Peter 3:7 when we went home again. I would continue to choose love.

There was one thing that went wrong with my experiment, however. It's something Evelyn and I laugh about today. On the last night at our cottage, preparing for bed, I saw Evelyn staring at me with the saddest expression.

"What's the matter, honey?" I asked.

"Tom," she said, sniffling, then looking pleadingly into my eyes. "Do you know something I don't?"

"What do you mean?"

"Well...that check-up I had several weeks ago...our doctor... did he tell you something about me...Tom, you've been so good to me, honey...am I dying, Tom?"

It took a minute for it all to sink in. Then I burst out laughing.

"No, honey," I said, wrapping her in my arms, "you're not dying, but I'm just starting to live!"

A Love Story

Love is made of...
The happy glow that sharing brings,
A secret smile, a small surprise,
A special look in a loved one's eyes.
Comfort given, interest shown,
Quiet moments spent alone—
It's the "little things," small and sweet,
That make a love story complete.

UNKNOWN

Class Act

BY MEGAN FELT

Once, I wanted to be a pharmacist when I grew up. I saw myself behind the drugstore counter in my small Kansas town, helping people like my mom, who was diagnosed with cancer my freshman year of high school. I would've done it except for something else that happened that year—something that changed my life. At a time when death and loss seemed about to claim my family, I found out about a woman who had fought, and sometimes cheated, death with a courage that still rings like a clarion. The world had long ago forgotten her. But the moment I read her story, I realized even a small light can shine in the darkness and not be overcome. She helped me find my own light. And she taught me that anyone, even a farm girl from Kansas, can live a life wider than the biggest, bluest prairie sky.

It all started with a history project, one activity I didn't drop when Mom got sick. At the beginning of the year at Uniontown High School, three friends—Elizabeth Cambers, Sabrina Coons, and Jessica Shelton—and I signed up for National History Day, a contest in which more than half a million students compete to create the most compelling presentation of a historical topic. We made our project a one-act play about the Holocaust, mostly because we liked the idea of learning about a time and place so far from our own. I'd spent my whole life on the farm, where my parents grew corn, beans, and wheat and ran about three hundred head of cattle. As far as we knew, no Jewish person had ever attended Uniontown. It was a small school. There were only twenty-nine kids in our graduating class.

We asked one of Uniontown's history teachers, Norm Conard, to help us find an actual person to research. Mr. Conard was the school's National History Day coordinator—and a big reason I hadn't pulled out of the contest. He was one of those teachers who can get students excited about anything. His classroom was big and airy, with murals on the walls and kids always hanging around, talking history. Leafing through a stack of old newspaper and magazine clippings he gave us, we came across an article from *U.S.News & World Report.* "The Other Schindlers," it was called, referring to the movie *Schindler's List*, about a Polish businessman who helped more than 1,200 Jews avoid death camps. The article described a half dozen people who'd also saved Jews but had never been recognized. One name jumped out: "Irena Sendlerowa. Social Worker. Smuggled more than 2,500 children to safety from the Warsaw Ghetto." To preserve their names, she wrote them on sheets of paper and buried them in jars out in her garden.

We looked at each other. Twenty-five hundred? That was a thousand more than Oskar Schindler had saved. I tried to picture this woman, the children she'd rescued. How had she gotten them out of the ghetto? Why had she risked her life? "I doubt anyone's ever heard of her," Elizabeth said. "She probably died in obscurity. This is going to be a great project."

But our excitement quickly dimmed. Irena was unknown for a reason. There was no information about her. We combed through books, newspapers, the Internet, even went to the Midwest Center for Holocaust Education in Kansas City. Nothing. There was a brief mention on the website of an organization called The Jewish Foundation for the Righteous. But when we wrote to them, their reply was vague.

One afternoon we were working on computers in Mr. Conard's room when Elizabeth suddenly sat back. "You guys!" she cried. "It's an e-mail from the Foundation for the Righteous." We rushed over.

"Dear Ms. Cambers," the e-mail read. And went on to apologize for taking so long to respond. The next sentence leapt out at us. "If you wish more information about Irena Sendlerowa, we recommend you contact her directly. She is currently ninety years old, living in a small apartment in Warsaw." Irena was alive! We immediately wrote a letter, explaining who we were and enclosing our play, pictures of us, and three dollars for return postage. Would she get it? Could she read English? Would she respond?

I needed her to respond. Irena had become one of the few happy things I had to talk about at home, where Mom was sick and Dad worked late getting all the farm chores done. Irena was becoming a beacon for me that needed to stay lit.

A few weeks later a note came to my English class instructing me to report to Mr. Conard's room. I got there and saw him with Elizabeth, Sabrina, and Jessica—holding a letter with a Polish postmark. "Is it...?" I asked.

"It is," said Elizabeth. We gazed at the envelope, festooned with heart-shaped stickers and addressed in old-fashioned, looping handwriting. We tore it open and...it was written in Polish. We looked despairingly at Mr. Conard. "We'll find a translator at the University of Kansas," he said. We faxed the translator the letter and, page by page, it came back to us. We tore the first sheet out of the fax machine.

"To my dear and beloved girls, very close to my heart," Irena began. And she proceeded to tell us everything—how she'd talked her way into the ghetto on the pretext of checking for typhus, then smuggled babies out in streetcars, wrapping them like parcels. She described her fear, the agony of persuading parents to part with their children, the bittersweet feeling of arranging an adoption. She had assumed she'd die when the Gestapo arrested her in 1943 and fractured her legs and feet during an interrogation. But members of the Polish under-ground bribed a guard to set her free, and she lived to retrieve the children's names she had buried in her garden. She tried to reunite them with their parents after the war, but so many had died. She was flattered by our play but insisted she was no hero. "I did what anyone would have done." She thanked us for the three dollars, which she gave to a Catholic boys' home. "I hope you will stay in touch," she concluded. I read that letter many times, especially those haunting words near the end: "I did what anyone would have done." Was that true? Would I have done the same thing? How could I, a farm girl with a sick mom who spent most evenings doing dishes and making sure her little brother finished his homework? Irena had blazed out against a horrible darkness. My own life felt pretty dark, especially when Mom came home from chemo. But I didn't feel very courageous.

With Irena's letter, we made it to the National History Day finals in College Park, Maryland. We didn't win, but we did get some coverage in a local Kansas newspaper. Soon, civic organizations were calling, asking us to perform our play, *Life in a Jar*. We were reluctant at first, until we realized Irena would want us to educate others—and we could use the performances to raise money for her. We took props and traveled to local schools, churches, and Rotary clubs, passing a jar for donations. After one performance in Kansas City, a Jewish businessman called. "Would you like to go to Warsaw to meet Irena?" he asked. "I'll pay your way if you come back and talk to my businessmen's association about what you find."

In May 2001 we were on a plane for Warsaw—the other girls, my mom, whose cancer had gone into remission, and me. When we landed, the Polish press mobbed us. An American correspondent for a Polish newspaper had written a story about our trip. Cameramen followed us to an apartment, where Irena, weak from high blood pressure, sat waiting. We walked down a hall, heard a tiny voice, and there she was, not five feet tall, calling our names. We ran to her and hugged her, everyone crying. Feeling the frailness of her body, an exhilarating rush came over me. Irena was a hero. But she was also, just as she'd insisted, a person like anyone else. That's what made her special. Perhaps her acts of goodness were comparatively small—2,500 saved out of six million killed. But here we were, still feeling their effect. If she, by herself, could do so much, why couldn't I?

I'm grown now, but I'm still asking that question. I didn't end up becoming a pharmacist. I helped found a nonprofit organization instead, one that shows schools how to do what we did at Uniontown. It's a vocation I could never have imagined. But that's what happens when God moves in your life. A light shines in the dark. And nothing is ever the same again.

Seeds of Love

*Live for today but hold your hands open
to tomorrow. Anticipate the future and its
changes with joy. There is a seed of God's
love in every event, every circumstance...
in which you may find yourself.*

BARBARA JOHNSON

My Biggest Catch

BY SUSAN KARAS

Fishing. Lots of men love it. If you're a man in my husband Bruce's family, it's mandatory. "It's how I grew up," Bruce told me back when we first started dating. I couldn't help asking about all of the photos in his parents' den of him and the rest of the Karas men proudly holding up dead fish. "Dad's father taught him to love it, and my dad taught me," Bruce said.

There were fishing photos of Bruce's mom on the wall too. "Mom's a real sportswoman," Bruce had said, pointing to a shot of her in beat-up jeans, a big floppy sun hat, and the obligatory fish. "She loves fishing almost as much as Dad and I do."

A note of affectionate pride drifted through Bruce's voice. I decided if I was going to win his heart completely I'd better turn into a sportswoman too, every bit as comfortable on a pitching boat with a bucket of bait beside me as I was at home in my own kitchen.

It was a bright June morning when Bruce took me out on his beloved thirty-foot sportfishing boat, the *Canyon Fever*. *This wasn't so bad*, I thought as we cruised down Mud Creek toward the open water of Moriches Bay on Long Island Sound. I'd never seen Long Island from the water before. It was beautiful, with gorgeous homes clustered against the shoreline. *I can't believe how nervous I was about doing this. I'm a natural!*

Things changed when we hit the bay. As soon as Bruce passed the channel buoy he pushed the throttle forward, and I flew off my seat.

"Can't you go a little slower?" I shouted over the roar of the engine.

"Not if we want to get to the fishing spot before dark!" Bruce shouted back, a big grin on his face. Looking around, I suddenly realized how many other boats were with us on the water. Half the population of Long Island seemed to be out there. My mouth went dry. How did people keep from crashing into each other with no lanes to stay in, no signs to follow?

By the time we dropped anchor I was so shaky I could barely hold my rod. Watching the sun climb above the horizon, I realized that I'd left my own big floppy hat back on the kitchen counter. I'd be baked to a crisp by the time we got home. What else could go wrong?

I got my answer in the form of a queasy feeling—one that started in the pit of my stomach and grew stronger with each slap of the waves against the boat. Suddenly that bucket of bait next to me didn't smell just a little bad. It smelled worse than I'd ever imagined anything could.

"You feeling okay, sweetie?" Bruce asked me. "You're looking a little green around the gills."

"I'll be fine," I whispered, trying desperately to get the words out while keeping my breakfast in.

Half an hour later we were speeding back to Mud Creek, with Bruce's Saturday of fishing ruined by his landlubber wife.

"Want to give it another try tomorrow?" he said gamely the following Friday night.

"That's okay," I said. "You go have fun."

The whole time Bruce was gone that Saturday, I couldn't stop thinking about what a failure I was. It would have been a lot easier if Bruce had been a football nut. I could just plop down next to him and watch a little of the game. The living room couch didn't buck back and forth and make you sick. But now I moped around the house, sick with disappointment. Finally, in desperation, I turned to prayer. *I don't want to be one of those wives who keeps busy while their husbands pursue what they really love. I want to share Bruce's passion. Help me find a way to be at Bruce's side. I'll do anything.*

The next Saturday I accompanied Bruce again, this time armed with a seasickness remedy. But I still got sick. I tried every brand on the market—and a couple of homemade remedies to boot. None worked. Every fishing trip ended the same way, with me hanging over the side of the boat till Bruce turned around and brought us in. Some sportswoman. Some wife.

Fishing season came and went, and I had to accept that I would never be the kind of wife that Bruce's mom was. Then one Saturday Bruce came home and announced that he'd met a couple named Bette and Frank at the new marina where he was docking *Canyon Fever*.

"Real nice," he said. "Real boat people. They throw a barbecue at the marina every Thursday. I told them we might show up next week."

"So it's a boating get-together?"

Bruce gave me a wry smile. "The boats are docked, sweetie. The barbecue's on dry land. What do you say?"

All the other wives probably fished with their husbands, and I'd stick out like a landlubber more than ever. But I could tell Bruce wanted me to go. "Okay," I said. "I'll make a couple of side dishes to bring along."

On Thursday afternoon I fussed over my outfit for a solid hour before finally piling into the car with Bruce and a cooler full of sodas, two big bowls of my trademark potato salad, and a stack of prime steaks just for good measure. The marina was packed when we got there, the air thick with the smoke from a line of grills set by some picnic tables covered in cheerful checkered cloths.

"You must be Susan!" a woman in bright blue Capris said. "I'm Bette. I've been so looking forward to meeting you!" Her husband came over and joined us. "That's my boat there, right next to your husband's," he said, pointing out at the water. "Don't they look beautiful?"

I looked out at the harbor full of tranquilly bobbing boats. He was right. They did look beautiful. From here, with my feet planted firmly on solid ground.

"At least from a distance!" Bruce said, finishing my thought. "My wife just doesn't have the stomach to go out on one." He threw his arm around me.

"That's okay," Bette said. "Not all wives love fishing."

"They don't?" I asked.

"Oh, heavens, no," Bette said, laughing.

One of the ladies who'd joined us wrinkled her nose. "Who wants to spend all Saturday on a cramped little boat that smells like squid guts?"

Some of the other wives laughed—apparently in agreement. All at once it became clear to me. Maybe my seasickness was God's way of telling me to stop trying to be someone I wasn't. Maybe all I needed to do was let Bruce love me the way I am—just the way I loved him. *Stop trying so hard, Susan,* an inner voice told me, loud and clear. *Just be who you are.*

Bruce and I got to be regulars at the Thursday night barbecue. We even have a picture of us together there hanging on our den wall along with Bruce's fishing pictures. Actually, I guess you could say that it's a fishing picture too, because it shows Bruce and me with our best catches ever—each other.

An Ocean of Love

*Love grows from our capacity to give
what is deepest within ourselves and also
receive what is the deepest within another person.
The heart becomes an ocean strong
and deep, launching all on its tide.*

UNKNOWN

The Captain's Decision

BY SCOTT SOUTHWORTH

Christmas 2003. An orphanage in the middle of war-torn Baghdad. I was standing by a courtyard play area, talking to one of the nuns who cared for the children about a nine-year-old boy named Ala'a I'd gotten to know—okay, come to love—since my National Guard unit had started visiting the orphanage a few months before. Out of the blue, the nun said matter-of-factly, "A year from now we will have to move Ala'a to a government-run orphanage. He will be too big for us to care for him."

Immediately I pictured Ala'a, so tiny I could wrap my thumb and forefinger around his leg. My stomach felt like I was about to go into combat. This orphanage was run by nuns from Mother Teresa's Missionaries of Charity. It was an oasis of peace in a city of chaos. I knew about that government-run orphanage. It would be a death sentence for a boy like Ala'a, with cerebral palsy, no known relations and an American National Guard soldier for a best friend. I didn't even think. "Then I'll adopt him," I blurted out.

The nun looked at me, surprised. I was stunned too. What had I just said? Had I really offered to adopt a disabled child?

From a war zone? I was a workaholic thirty-year-old bachelor with a career back home in Wisconsin. A career I might not even make it home to. Even if I did, what would I do with a nine-year-old? I didn't know how to raise kids. I'd only graduated law school a few years before. I lived with my parents, commuting seventy-five miles each way to Madison, the state capital, where I was chief of staff for my hometown state legislator.

I remembered my first day at the orphanage when Ala'a had pulled himself across the floor with his hands, planted himself right in front of me, and smiled the most electric smile I'd ever seen. It didn't take him long to start calling me Baba, Arabic for father. We'd sit and talk—he'd learned crisply accented English from the Indian nuns—and walk around and play games in his wheelchair. Sometimes he'd tell me about his prayers. His favorite place in the orphanage was the sisters' small, simple chapel. He prayed all the time, as if he knew God was listening. Not like I prayed. Not like any grown-up I knew prayed. How could I let him go? And yet—how could I possibly take him?

The nun drifted away, and soon it was time to leave. I said good-bye and, that night, lay in my bunk, mind racing. Outside, sounds of Baghdad's Green Zone—our military police unit was headquartered in a bombed-out former Baathist Party country club—hummed in the winter desert air. Had I just made a promise I couldn't keep? I didn't do that sort of thing. I'd been raised to honor my word. And yet—already I could hear my mom, worrying that combat stress was pushing me over the edge. Dad, who'd been in Vietnam, would understand. He sometimes talked of the kids he'd wanted to rescue from his own war zone long ago. But he was also committed to my public-service career. As committed as I was. I knew what he'd say: "Be very careful, son. You don't know what you're getting into." Praying for guidance, for an answer, for something, I finally fell asleep.

By the time I saw Ala'a again the next week, I'd sent e-mails, telling friends and family what I planned to do. The responses read as expected. "Take a little time to think this through," Mom suggested. Dad and I didn't even discuss it.

A friend who was a single mom sent a long e-mail spelling out the difficulties of raising a child, the way it consumes all your time, the emotional commitment.

At the orphanage, Ala'a let me know he wanted to go to America. The nuns too said that all of the kids frequently talked about going there.

Every time I talked to my parents and my friends, I cautiously brought up Ala'a. They all knew if anyone would do something like this, it would be me. Still, they urged me to be careful.

Driving Baghdad's wary streets, talking to the Iraqi police officers it was our mission to train, I had thoughts that kept revolving in my head like an endless slide show. One moment I saw Ala'a, so bright and funny, so faithful, so vulnerable. And then I saw myself, everything I owned packed in a few boxes in my parents' basement. My car, a Chrysler Concorde, not exactly wheelchair-ready. My salary as a state legislative aide, not nearly enough to support a family.

Back at the orphanage, I talked with an Iraqi doctor who helped supervise the children. "So, you're really serious," she said. I nodded. She looked at me more closely. "Captain Scott, do you realize how difficult it is to take care of a child with cerebral palsy?" I tried giving an optimistic answer. Quickly, she set me straight. "It is not like coming to an orphanage two times a week," she said. "Ala'a will be your responsibility every minute of every day. You will have to feed him, dress him, get him up, and put him to bed. You will have to help him in the bathroom. Every day, Captain Scott. It is truly a heavy responsibility. Are you sure you're ready for it?"

I looked at her and swallowed, trying to nod.

That night I lay awake in my bunk, utterly dejected. I needed a straightforward answer from God. I needed a miracle to make this work. I was thankful for the doctor's words, but I had expected her to be as excited as I was. Instead, all she had pointed out were the challenges of taking care of a child like Ala'a. Trying to figure out all of this, I envisioned myself in heaven, explaining to Ala'a why I had decided not to adopt him. "Baba," he asked, "why didn't you take me home with you?" I stammered through a series of excuses.

"Well, Ala'a, you see, I had my career, and—" I sputtered out. The words sounded excruciatingly lame. I felt God's patient eyes on me. I tried another. "Ala'a, I don't know anything about taking care of a child with cerebral palsy. I have no experience with that. I'm sure someone else would do a better job. I don't make much money!" I cried. "I drive a Concorde! I have a seventy-five-mile commute!" The excuses became increasingly pathetic. I realized just how ashamed I'd feel if I really did leave him there in Baghdad. I would feel guilty for the rest of my life. I didn't need to think about my decision anymore.

It took seven months to get Ala'a out of Iraq. My tour of duty ended in July 2004, and I spent the next six months at home working with the Iraqi government and an immigration lawyer, bombarding the U.S. embassy with my requests.

In the fall I was elected district attorney in my county. In February 2005 I flew to Amman, Jordan, then to Baghdad, where a translator from the orphanage had driven Ala'a through the city's violent streets. They hadn't told him I was coming to get him, in case insurgents found out. I walked through the airport—the same airport I had seen derelict right after the invasion—and there he was, in a wheelchair, surrounded by the orphanage sisters. For a moment we were silent, too astonished by the journey the two of us were about to take. Then I went over and held him in my arms.

We flew to Chicago, then Wisconsin. I drove him to the apartment I had recently rented and showed him his bedroom, decorated by my mom. There were toys, books, an American flag, my old chest of drawers. He grinned his ecstatic grin. I grinned too. Laughed, in fact. I had spent months wondering whether

I could really do this—me, a law-school graduate, American soldier, now prosecutor. All that, and it took an Iraqi orphan who couldn't walk to show me what real faith, real strength, real *love* looks like.

I'm still not sure. Did I adopt Ala'a? Or did he adopt me?

Extravagant Love

Jesus' message is just as powerful today as it was then. Don't miss it: "There is a time for risky love. There is a time for extravagant gestures. There is a time to pour out your affections on one you love. And when the time comes—seize it, don't miss it."

MAX LUCADO

The Art of Compassion

BY MICHAEL DAUBE

Two little children in Calcutta, India, a teeming city of millions, most of them poor. Urchins, they would have been called in a Dickens novel. The boy maybe eight, the girl twelve or so. They might have been brother and sister. I don't know.

They tugged at my jacket as I walked down a packed street. "Sir, sir, spare some money?" the girl asked. I tried to move on. Because of the crushing poverty, begging was practically an industry in Calcutta. It was 1988. I was twenty-four, a struggling artist just out of Brooklyn's Pratt Institute. Like generations of young people before me, I traveled to India in search of something vaguely spiritual. I just wasn't sure what.

The kids persisted. The boy thrust up his fingers. "Please, sir," he said. His fingers were mangled stubs. The girl held her hands up too. They were the same. I wasn't shocked. This was standard begging strategy, and I couldn't give what I didn't have.

"We're lepers," the girl cried. I didn't know whether to believe them. I quickened my step. So did they. What did they want from me? I was just a scraggly young American with a backpack. There were many more prosperous-looking tourists all around. "Come and see where we go for lunch," the boy said, keeping up.

I thought about how I must look to them. A fairly clean pair of jeans and a backpack must've seemed so affluent. "Okay," I said, not sure why. Maybe my conscience had something to do with it. How could I turn them away?

They led me down a back street to a drab stucco building. The girl reached up and pulled on a bell. The door opened. A nun appeared. "Welcome," she said. From within I heard voices—children's voices. I was led into a room lined with about twenty cots. "This is our orphanage," said a nun. "Some, like these two, just eat here." Maybe it was the look on my face that said I was losing my heart to these kids. "Let me take you to meet the sister who runs our place," the nun said.

She showed me to an unadorned room off the main quarters. It was empty, save for a plain wooden table, two chairs, a bare lightbulb hanging over the table, and a curtain for a door. One of the walls was inscribed with a prayer by St. Francis. A moment passed. I studied the prayer. There was nothing else to do. A nun wearing a white head shawl bordered in blue finally stepped through the curtain. She was short and energetic with a remarkable aura about her. "I'm Mother Teresa," she said.

I'd never heard of her. But I could see she was smart and charismatic. She drew me right in. I'd come to India to travel and soak up its culture until my money ran out. So I was shocked to hear myself say, "Could I stay here and help you?"

Mother Teresa looked at me appraisingly, then spoke. "Are you a doctor?" she asked, almost sharply. "A nurse? A psychologist? Do you have any medical training?"

"No," I said.

"Then how can you help us?"

How could I argue with this tiny nun? All I had to offer was my middle-class American sympathy. What they needed were doctors and medicine and therapy, not pity. I'm sure I looked crestfallen. Mother Teresa spoke in a soft tone. "We can use you in Kali temple," she said. It was a home for the dying, she explained, that she'd established in a Hindu temple in a poor district of Calcutta. "The only skills you need there are gentleness and patience." I stayed in the old temple for about a month, caring for those in the last days of life. I washed and fed them, and sat and talked with those who could speak.

"I used to be a schoolteacher," said one. "I was a government worker," said another. They spoke with honesty and with poignancy—mostly about how they had entered adulthood hoping to better their lives and the lives of their families. "But I had so little money," said the schoolteacher. "The lack of opportunity just beats you down," the government worker said. Remorse and sadness seemed to shroud them. Each day some would die and others would walk through the door and take their place. Each day I would ask myself, *Is this what I sought when I came to India?*

At night I retreated to my room. With my money dwindling, without knowing anyone, there was little to do but sit and think.

Here I was just starting out and I was spending my time with people at the end of their lives. The work was hard, but it spoke to me. One thing I knew: when I returned to the comforts of home, India would never be far from my mind.

Broke, I headed back to the States and settled into an artist's loft in Jersey City, doing sculpture and helping other, better-known artists with their large installations. Nights, though, it wasn't just my art I was thinking about. The images of the kids, of those dying people, of Mother Teresa, played in my head. Art is meant to be inspiring. But I didn't see how my talent would better the life of any of those I'd left behind in India. If I would've thought to pray I would have pleaded for guidance.

I didn't need to. One day I was rummaging through an abandoned storage space on the floor beneath my studio loft. I was searching for odds and ends I might use for a sculpture I was working on—a series of wooden panels with everyday objects. I spotted an old frame buried in a pile of junk. I yanked it out. It was a painting—a portrait. I recognized the man in the picture: Ossie Clark, a well-known designer from the 1960s. But more important, I recognized the style of the artist and the signature in the bottom right-hand corner: DH. It was a long-lost work by David Hockney, one of the most important artists of the latter half of the twentieth century!

I took it to Sotheby's, the famous art auction house. The appraiser offered me eighteen thousand dollars, more money than I'd ever had at one time. Friends asked what I was going to do with it. Move to a bigger studio? Be free to create more art? The odd thing was, I knew instantly. I packed a bag and flew to see Mother Teresa. Again I stood in the orphanage, in that same barren room. She walked through the curtain exuding that same energetic strength.

"Mother Teresa," I said, "I've come back." I explained the circumstances of my return.

She studied me carefully. "So many young people like you cluster in the cities. You should go to a rural area, where there are so few volunteers and so much need. The Lord will show you."

The train took ten and a half hours to get to Orissa, the poorest state in India. I stopped at a destitute village named Juanga. I sat under a shade tree where villagers gathered and, with the help of an interpreter, asked what they needed. "Doctors," said one. "Medicine," said another. "People die because there are no pharmacies."

There, under the tree, the answer came to me, as if this Lord that Mother Teresa spoke about had whispered in my ear: *Build them a hospital. And staff it.*

It took three years, all of my seed money plus a ton of fundraising and the sweat of a lot of locals, but in 1996 we opened a thirty-bed hospital with round-the-clock physician care. The day we opened, everyone in Juanga and the surrounding villages came. Some had stitched a huge net of lotus flowers and jasmine, and draped it over the building. That first month, we treated more than a thousand people, many who had never been to a doctor. "You don't know how much this means," a farmer, whose wife had been bedridden for months for want of penicillin, said.

I returned home and established Citta (Sanskrit for "compassionate mind"), a charitable organization that provides assistance to destitute communities around the world. We've opened hospitals, schools, women's centers, and orphanages in rural India, Nepal, and Mexico. Today, I spend much time traveling between them and back to the States.

I started out an artist. I still am in a sense. Like great art, helping others inspires. It empowers both the giver and the receiver and appeals to a deep human beauty. Compassion, I learned from Mother Teresa, illuminates the soul. It may be the greatest art of all.

The Art of Loving

Whether we are poets or parents or teachers or artists or gardeners, we must start where we are and use what we have. In the process of creation and relationship, what seems mundane and trivial may show itself to be holy, precious, part of a pattern.

LUCI SHAW

A Good Guy

BY DAWN KUZEL

Friday night. It was getting to be my least favorite night of the week. At least on weeknights it wasn't a crime for a twenty-four-year-old single woman to stay home. But on a Friday evening if I plopped down in the den with Mom after dinner she'd say, "You won't find the man of your dreams by sitting home with me."

I knew that was true, but there wasn't a single man who interested me at the fish, meat, and poultry warehouse where I worked. And I wasn't crazy about meeting guys at bars or clubs. In fact, maybe I'd just given up. That Friday night I sat in my room, depressed. I'd looked everywhere for the man of my dreams. I knew my mom was praying for me, but I said a prayer for myself too: *God, if You don't want me to be single the rest of my life, You will need to bring the man to me, because I can't find him!*

The phone rang. It was my friend Jodi. "Get dressed. We're going out," she said. "There's a party."

"Forget it," I told her. "I'd rather stay in and rent a movie."

Jodi nagged and nagged until she finally gave up. "Okay, swing by and get me," she said, "and we'll pick out a good romantic movie and cry our eyes out together."

It was cold and wet. We checked out four video stores before we could agree on a movie. Something funny and sweet where the guy and the girl end up together. If only real life could work out that way. It's not like I wanted some Hollywood hunk for a boyfriend. I just wanted someone who was polite and thoughtful and actually listened to me instead of talking about himself the whole time. A good guy. Was that too much to ask?

We were driving home when all of a sudden I heard the wail of a siren behind us and saw red lights flashing in my rearview mirror. "Oh no," I groaned. A ticket. That's all I needed.

I pulled over. An unmarked SUV parked behind me. I rolled down the window and waited. The cop bent down to the window. "Miss," he asked, "do you realize you were going fifty-six miles per hour in a forty-mile-an-hour zone?" At least he had a nice deep voice.

"No, officer, I didn't," I said, hoping he'd let me off the hook.

He asked for my license and registration and headed back to his car. It took him awhile to return. "Sorry for the delay," he said, "but I had to write up two citations. Your inspection sticker has expired." Then he handed me the citations to sign. "You can request a hearing if you want to, or just send it in. Thank you and have a nice evening." He turned and walked away.

"Can you believe that?" I asked Jodi, who slumped down in the front seat as if she didn't want to be seen with a lawbreaker. "He couldn't have given me just one ticket?" I moaned.

I was so sick to my stomach I could barely concentrate on the movie that night. Ask for a hearing. I cringed at the thought, but

I knew I had to do it. No way in the world could I afford to pay all those fines. I'd just bought the car. Was it my fault that the previous owners hadn't had it inspected?

I showed up at the hearing, my head spinning, my stomach in knots. What had I gotten myself into? I looked for the officer in his uniform—admittedly, he wasn't bad looking, but then it was dark that night. To my surprise he strolled into the magistrate's office in civilian clothes: a crisp white shirt, pale pink tie, black pants, and a long camel hair overcoat. What a sharp dresser. He gave me a pleasant smile and nod. I glanced at his ring finger. Bare. Unmarried. *What if...* I thought. I stopped myself. I mean, the man was about to testify against me! He'd throw the book at me!

The hearing didn't last long. "Guilty," the magistrate said. I was ushered into another office and asked to sign some papers. I reached into my purse for a pen. All at once I burst into tears. I felt like such a loser! My shoulders started shaking. *Lord, don't let me fall apart.* But I couldn't stop myself.

Then I heard that soothing baritone voice. I turned and there he was. "Dawn," he said, "are you all right?" His face was kind and caring. His name was Carl and we talked for a while—until I felt better—then he walked me to my car. We shook hands and said good-bye.

The minute I walked in the door at home Mom asked me what had happened. "I lost," I said, smiling. "They threw the book at me!"

"So, why are you smiling?" Mom hesitated then, with a sparkle in her eye, added, "You know, God does have a wonderful sense of humor."

All that week I thought of Carl. A little upset still, but I couldn't help recalling how kind he was, how good-looking. I knew it was silly of me. After all, I only knew him from the night he pulled me over and from our meeting in the magistrate's office. I'd seen him for all of forty-five minutes, max. But there was something about the way he'd squeezed my hand when we said good-bye, the comforting look in his eyes when he saw me crying. Was it possible that he was the man who was meant for me? If only I could see him again, if only we could get to know each other a little bit better.

One evening my friend and I returned to the video store. I was checking out the rack of romantic comedies when I heard a voice—a voice I had been hearing inside my head for weeks. "Hi, Dawn." I turned. It was Carl. In uniform. Still good-looking. Really good-looking.

"Carl," I said, nearly dropping the videos. We chatted for a little longer—*O God*, I prayed, *why doesn't he ask me out?*—then he said good-bye and headed outside. My friend and I paid for our videos and rushed outside too. In the parking lot I looked over at his SUV. The window rolled down.

"Dawn, can you come here for a minute?" Carl asked. I walked over. "I still feel bad about giving you those tickets. Can I take you out to dinner?"

That date we went to Eat 'n' Park for dinner—my favorite—and then to a movie. Afterward, we drove to the Mt. Washington district, which overlooks all of downtown Pittsburgh.

Carl turned out to be just what I thought he was—a good guy. Friday nights I wasn't a homebody anymore. Mom called him my answer to prayer. Today, I call him my husband. And if you ask me how I met him, I'd tell you that you would never believe it.

Surprised by Love

There is no surprise more magical than the surprise of being loved; it is God's finger on a person's shoulder.

CHARLES MORGAN

Caregiver of the Year

BY ALEC ROGERS

My days in retirement had started to blur together. Oh, they were pleasant enough—summer days spent lolling away up at our lake house, puttering on the boat, visiting with our kids and grandkids. But lately I'd felt this grinding sameness. I was growing bored. And to think I'd looked forward to retirement. No boss to answer to. No workaday rat race. I'd had a good career as a plant pathologist for a big agricultural chemical company. My work had helped people. Maybe I got out too early, I thought. Maybe I still have something to give. I felt a dreariness I'd never expected. Once or twice I opened the paper to the want ads. I read them with nostalgia. "Scientist needed. Must be a self-starter." Too late, I thought. My self-starting days were over.

One day my eye fell on a small ad that said "Be a caregiver." Just three words. I'd helped nurse both my parents through their final, long illnesses. It had been rough. Not just seeing them become elderly but trying to keep their lives going on a daily basis. Trips to the bank, the pharmacy, the grocery store. I frequently wished I had help. Now I read closer. That's exactly what this agency, Home Instead Senior Care, was advertising for. People who could help out homebound seniors.

I clipped the ad and put it into my pocket. Maybe it was God saying, *Alec, get a grip. This is what you need.* Oh, yeah? Caregiving is hard work. Why would I want to sit at the bedside of some stranger or run errands for him? I was bored enough doing errands for myself. Yet, despite all my good arguments, I called the number. Within a few months I had my first assignment. A marine suffering from terminal cancer (I'll call him Donnie) needed company and care.

Okay, I'll give this a try. If you think I was welcomed with open arms, think again. Donnie practically threw me out of his house. "I don't need anyone's help," the old leatherneck snapped. I apologized to his wife and came back the next day...and the next. If he could be stubborn, so could I. I discovered what he liked was to talk. So I read him the paper and we'd "discuss" politics, the arts, sports. He'd get ornery. That's when I'd retreat to the kitchen and whip up a batch of his favorite stew. For six months, until he died, I visited him four hours a day, every day. "Where's Alec?" he always asked his wife toward the end. And mostly I was with him, as much as I could be. My days took on a new sense of purpose that retirement had drained from them. It wasn't so much a second career as a second life. What had been missing was the simple act of helping others.

I've had fourteen other clients since Donnie, most recently, a prominent oral surgeon. When we first met he was bedridden and so depressed he hardly cared about living. But one thing he loved was cars. "I've seen some pretty nice ones outside," I said, meaning the ones in his garages. Finally I coaxed him into a wheelchair and outside. "Ah," he said with some surprise, "the fresh air." I felt I'd won as big a victory as I'd ever won in the lab at work. The funny thing is, what I do for my clients isn't much different from the mundane chores I did for myself. I run to the post office, make bank deposits, shop at the grocery, do the laundry, cook a dinner. But I do those chores for someone else, and that makes all the difference in the world.

Choose Love

*How you do something
and the attitude with which you do it
are usually even more important
than what you do....
Often we have no choice about doing things,
but we can always choose how to do them.
And that...can make all the difference.*

DR. NORMAN VINCENT PEALE

Together

BY JERRY HUNT

The last thing I remember is the car flipping over.

It was a Monday night. I was rushing home from work. Doris, my wife of just four months, had gotten home earlier to cook dinner. I was worried that I would spoil it by being late. I sped around a corner. I recall a sickening feeling of being airborne, of being out of control. Then nothingness. Police said the car rolled five times before coming to rest on its roof in the high grass of a roadside ditch. I didn't regain consciousness until Friday.

"How bad is it, Doc?" I insisted weakly from my hospital bed. I needed to know. I didn't want to wait for bad news.

The doctor gave it to me straight. "Jerry," he said, his voice just audible above the hum of all the medical machinery I was hooked up to, "you are paralyzed from the chest down. You will probably never walk again. I'm sorry. It could have been worse."

Worse? I wondered as panic overcame me. How could it be any worse?

The doctor pressed an X-ray up to the light. "Your spinal cord was damaged here, at this vertebra," he explained, pointing with a pen to the crushed bone. "Had you broken the vertebra just one up, you'd have lost use of your arms too. You might not have survived."

I closed my eyes. Paralyzed. Memories of my older brother flooded my mind. Larry too had been doomed to a wheelchair after a crash, his body useless from the neck down. He died eighteen years later.

And what about Doris? How will she adjust to suddenly having a disabled husband?

Just then Doris rushed through the door. Tears filled her eyes as she gently cradled my head in her arms. "Thank God you made it," she sighed.

That night I lay awake, restless. With every ounce of strength in my broken body I tried to wriggle my toes. I tried to will a movement in my leg, any movement. *Come on*, I concentrated. It was no use. I felt half dead, as if, at age thirty-four, life had just stopped from the chest down. Exhausted, I thought about Doris. A nurse had told me Doris was at the hospital day and night while I was unconscious. But would she stay with me over the long haul? I wondered. After all, we'd only been married a few months. Who could blame her for walking away from this situation? She was young, twenty-seven. She was active and full of energy. I'd seen how hard life had sometimes been for Larry. It was no picnic taking care of a full-grown man who couldn't take care of himself. Why should Doris let my rotten luck ruin her life as well?

When I awoke again Doris was at my bedside. "Hi," she said softly, smoothing my blanket. "It's good to sleep. You're getting your strength back."

"What strength?" I sighed. "You know what the doctor said."

"You were lucky, Jerry."

"Lucky? Do you feel lucky, Doris?"

She paused before answering, her eyes searching mine. "Yes," she finally said in a low, firm tone. "Yes I do. We're both very lucky, Jerry."

I knew she was right. I knew that I would just have to make the best of this situation. But still, in the weeks that followed, I had moments of despair and doubt. I wondered if a life in a wheelchair was even worth living. I worried about how we would pay for the hospitalization. The accident had occurred when I was without health insurance, and I knew we'd have to depend on outside sources to pay the medical costs that were mounting daily. I even thought that maybe it would have been better if I hadn't survived the accident.

One day Doris must have sensed how low I was feeling. She sat on the edge of the bed and took my hand.

"I'm going to tell you a story," she said. "When you were unconscious, the doctors were acting like you might not make it. I could sense their concern. I felt so helpless, so alone. How could I go on without my husband? I wandered in the hospital halls, trying to find an answer. One night I said to the nurses, 'I wish there was something I could do.' 'There is,' one said. 'Pray for him.'

"So I did. I prayed. I prayed like I hadn't prayed since I was a kid. I asked God to help us. After a while, I felt the fear draining away. The more I prayed, the more I sensed strength replacing fear. The night before you woke up I knew the Lord would help us face this no matter what. I found myself reciting my marriage vows outside your room. For better or for worse, in sickness and in health. Jerry, we're in this together. This happened to us, not just to you."

Suddenly I noticed how tired and drawn Doris looked. She was right. This had happened to us.

I spent the next two months in traction at High Point Regional Hospital. Every night, the whole night through, Doris was there by my side. She'd sleep in a chair in my room and bring a change of clothes with her. In the mornings she'd wash up, dress, go to her job as a cashier clerk, and then come back for the night. Eventually I was transferred to a rehabilitation hospital. They wouldn't let Doris stay overnight, but every evening after work she was there. I still had my moments of despair, of doubt, but they were fewer and farther between. And whenever they came, I prayed. I did everything the doctors and nurses asked of me. Three months passed and they said I was ready to leave.

"Oh, Jerry," cried Doris, "it'll be so wonderful to have you home again! I'm so excited!"

So was I. But I was also frightened. There would be no more nurses and doctors around the clock. We'd be on our own.

Doris had given up our house and moved our things into a small three-room apartment next door to her mother's. It was all we could afford on her salary. Each morning Doris would get up at the crack of dawn to get me ready for the day. It was quite an ordeal. Then she'd dash off to work.

Those first long days at home were tough. I wasn't used to being alone. I missed the staff at the hospital. I missed working at my job as an upholsterer. And sometimes I felt guilty over how hard Doris was working. She looked so tired, which was only natural; the alarm rang every two hours during the night, when she would rub my back and help me turn over in bed so I wouldn't develop sores. But if I ever felt myself slipping into self-pity, I'd remember what Doris said that day at the hospital: "Jerry, this happened to both of us." Still, I often wondered how she did it.

Then one night it became clear. I was watching her as she went about fixing me a snack and gathering some medicine that had to be taken with food. Suddenly it hit me.

It was love. Pure, simple, unquestioning love, the love that was the very heart of our commitment to each other. The kind of patient, devoted love between two people that swells with the passage of time, that grows stronger in the face of adversity. The only way to go on was to continue trusting that commitment, that love, and to hold ever fast to our faith in God to guide us.

When Doris brought my tray over I grasped her arm and pulled her to me. "I love you," I whispered.

One cold day Doris came home from work excited. "What you need, Jerry," she announced, "is one of those specially equipped vans for the disabled."

"Sure," I snorted indulgently. We'd talked before about getting a van. "But you don't even have enough gas money to get to work next week."

"Have faith," she beamed back.

Faith, I mused. Isn't faith, too, a kind of commitment, a two-way commitment between you and God?

A week or so later, we heard about a van for sale with a wheelchair lift. A young man had died of muscular dystrophy. His mother wanted very much to sell it to someone who could really use it. Still, even at a bargain price there was no way we could afford it.

"Sell that old boat of yours," suggested Doris slyly.

"No one buys boats in the winter," I insisted.

She put an ad in the paper anyway. The next day a fellow came out, took one look, and paid cash.

Our church then gave us a love offering to equip the van with an automatic door so I could get in and out by myself. Now that I could get around, I took a picture-framing course at our community college. Picture framing became my hobby, and now I even make a little money at it. Doris found a very good job as an insurance agent. Last year we moved into our own home on a beautiful three-acre wooded lot. There never seems to be enough time. When I'm not making frames, I'm bird-watching, cleaning house, or shopping. There's plenty that I can do.

It's been a number of years now that I've sat in this wheelchair, a number of the best years. But even under the best of circumstances, marriage is never easy. It takes work. It takes faith. It takes commitment.

One Sunday we came home from church and I lit a fire in the barbecue grill out on our spacious back patio. As Doris set the picnic table, I grilled some steaks over the charcoal flames. It was a beautiful afternoon. In the woods behind our house the birds were singing. Squirrels clamored through the tree branches. A warm, sweet breeze curled in from the south. Life was good.

When the steaks were ready, Doris asked me to say grace. I bowed my head. I couldn't help reflecting on how another day had gone by, and how with each passing day our commitment to each other deepens just a bit more. A commitment is like a tree that takes root. The longer it stands, the deeper the roots grow. And love is the richest growing soil.

For better or worse, we are in this together. Committed for life.

Love Lasts

Love is extravagant
in the price it is willing to pay,
the time it is willing to give,
the hardships it is willing to endure,
and the strength it is willing to spend.
Love never thinks in terms of "how little,"
but always in terms of "how much."
Love gives, love knows, and love lasts.

JONI EARECKSON TADA

The Five Reasons I Love My Life

BY DOLLY PARTON

I hear it from folks all the time: "Gosh, Dolly, you seem so happy!" Well, my smile's pretty hard to miss, considering I'm a gal who likes her lipstick—the redder, the better. Take it from me, though, the fancy makeup is just highlighting what's for real. And that's true happiness, the kind that comes from the inside. Lately I've been giving it some thought and I've come up with five things that make mine a happy life. Five things that make just about anyone's life joyous. Yours too, I bet.

1. I love my friends and family.

I grew up poor, so poor my daddy paid the doctor who delivered me with a sack of cornmeal. Yet my family was rich in so many ways too. Each and every one of us twelve kids knew we were precious in the sight of God and cherished by our mother and father. Maybe you've heard my song "Coat of Many Colors," about a girl who wears her coat of rags proudly. That came right out of my childhood in the Smoky Mountains in Tennessee. Someone gave us a box of rags, and Mama sewed them together to make a coat for me. The kids at school teased me, but I knew Mama put her love into every stitch. I felt proud to have that coat, and blessed.

Blessed as I felt the day I met Judy Ogle in third grade. My family had just moved to Caton's Chapel from another town in the Smoky Mountains. I walked into school, the new girl, too shy to make a peep. Until I noticed someone else quietly looking on. A girl with bright-green eyes and a copper-colored ponytail. Something told me to go over and say hi.

Years later, Judy and I haven't stopped talking. (Just ask my husband, Carl, who's always shaking his head at how we tie up the phone line.) If I get an idea for a tune while I'm picking at a guitar, Judy's there to write everything down before it goes out of my head. Whenever I need a dose of country air, Judy's there to drive out to the mountains with me. At the heart of every close friendship I have, there's what I discovered with Judy back in third grade—the magic of having someone in your life who understands where you're coming from and where you're going, who just knows.

2. I love what I do.

My daddy likes to say I was singing before I could talk. That might be a bit of a tall tale, but I can barely remember a time I wasn't making music. At age six, I was shaking the rafters at church. But our little country church could only fit so many people, and Sunday only came once a week. Mama said God had put His hand on me and given me my voice, so I decided He must have bigger plans for me.

Boy, did I want to be ready for them. I took up guitar at age seven, making my first instrument out of an old mandolin and two bass strings. I put on concerts right on our porch. To look the part of a glamorous singer, I used Mercurochrome for lipstick, crushed pokeberries for rouge, and a burnt match for mascara. I'd collect my brothers and sisters who were too young to run away, sit them down in the dirt, then get up on the porch and belt out songs into a tin can on a stick like I was at the Grand Ole Opry. If I couldn't round up any of my brothers and sisters, there were always the pigs and chickens to serenade.

I landed my first professional gig on the Cas Walker Radio Show in Knoxville (I'll tell you all about it later). I was ten. I've been making a living doing what I love ever since. Is it any wonder that I feel incredibly fortunate? Not to mention grateful.

3. I love to laugh.

People often compliment my voice, my songwriting, my business acumen, and yes, my distinctive fashion sense. But I've always felt that my greatest gift is my positive attitude and sense of humor (they go together like biscuits and gravy). It's like the Bible says, "A merry heart doeth good like medicine." My years with Carl have been one fun ride. He should hire himself out as a professional practical joker. I never know what he's going to pull next, but I do know it's going to leave me laughing.

I remember one concert in Louisville, Kentucky. My backup singers sounded kind of off. I glanced over my shoulder to see what was the matter. There was Carl at one of the microphones! And he had the audacity to wink at me. I decided to do him one better. I sauntered over to a policeman working security. "That man back there in the white shirt isn't part of our group," I told him. The cops hauled Carl away. It was all I could do not to crack up. (Don't worry, someone from our crew let the officers know who Carl was before they got too far.)

Having a live-in personal humor trainer like Carl is a big help. There are things I do on my own too, if my attitude needs adjusting. I visualize God holding me upside down and shaking all the negative stuff—fears, doubts, insecurities—right out of me. Try it. Ask God to turn you upside down! It's a surefire pick-me-up.

4. I love to pray.

Getting up close and personal with God is something I learned in His house. Not the way you'd expect, though. I used to explore the old church that my town, Caton's Chapel, was named after. It was a ruin—shattered windows, buckled floor, graffiti-splattered walls. Saturday nights teenagers partied there. Mama was aware of the not-so-wholesome goings-on and warned us to steer clear of the place. But for some reason I was drawn to it during daylight hours. I'd hunt for doodlebugs in the cool earth under the floorboards, daydream at the broken piano in the corner.

And I'd pray. I would tell God how I wanted to see the world that lay beyond the Smoky Mountains. To make it as a country music star and have a whole building full of folks to sing to. To do Mama and Daddy proud.

Was God listening? I couldn't quite tell. Then one day I was sitting in a pew, talking to Him, when suddenly, something changed in the very air around me. Something changed inside me too. I felt like I would bust with happiness. God was right there with me. I was absolutely sure. I didn't have to jump up and down or shout or even sing to get His attention. I could just whisper. He heard every word.

Something I would have done well to remember in the early 1980s, when I was going through the darkest time. Not that I had any real reason to be unhappy. I had a strong marriage, tons of family and friends, a well-established career. But a movie I'd made hadn't turned out well. I had some serious medical issues. Judy was going through a crisis of her own, so I couldn't lean on her like usual. And poor Carl was so worried about my health I didn't want to put any more on him. For the first time in my life, I felt all alone. Like no one was listening, not even God.

It was more an act of desperation than inspiration, but I grabbed for the only lifeline I could think of. The Bible. I sat down and read it cover to cover, a little every day. Pretty soon verses jumped out at me. Like that line in 1 Thessalonians that always had me stumped: "Pray without ceasing." How on earth was anyone going to do that? Coming out of that dark time, that's when I finally got what those words meant. No matter where I go or what I'm doing, a part of me is talking to God. And a part of God is listening.

5. I love you.

I believe God put the dream in my heart to become a country music performer so I could share the love He poured into my life with as many people as possible. I know you might think, *That's just Dolly being outrageous again,* but why else would God have let me discover what I did the first time I sang in front of an audience?

This gets back to that first gig I mentioned. I landed it thanks to my uncle, Bill Owens. I was ten, and he took me to Knoxville to meet Cas Walker, the host of a live music radio show. Cas said hello and stared down at me as if he expected me to say something back. Well, I did. I said, "Mr. Walker, I want to work for you." He shook my hand and said, "You're hired. A lot of people come to me and say, 'Mr. Walker, I want a job,' but you're the first one that ever said, 'I want to work.'"

The show was recorded in an auditorium that seated maybe sixty people. I walked up to the microphone and looked out at the audience. All those strangers! Whoa, this was a whole lot different from getting up in front of the pigs and chickens on our farm. The first notes were kinda squeaky. Pretty soon, though, the sheer joy of singing took over.

I finished with a flourish. Everyone clapped and stomped their feet. They wanted an encore, but I didn't have one. I looked over at Uncle Bill, and he mouthed, "Sing it again." So I did—and they cheered all over again, even louder. I never knew I could feel so close, so connected, to a bunch of strangers. That was the moment I fell in love with the people I sing for. With you. I've loved y'all ever since.

I am a happy person. That is my greatest blessing. It can be yours too. Think about it. Friends and family, work, laughter, prayer, love. They add up to joy. For you, for me, for anyone.

Free to Love

Those who love are borne on wings;
they run, and are filled with joy;
they are free and unrestricted.
They give all to receive all,
and they have all in all;
for beyond all things they rest in the One...
from whom streams all that is good.

THOMAS À KEMPIS

Remade

BY JOYCE BROTHERTON

The heart monitor beeped steadily. I pulled the thin hospital sheet up to my chin. My hands were freezing. An old saying popped into my mind—cold hands, warm heart. My heart felt like ice. No machine could measure the emotions I felt inside. I stroked the spot on my left ring finger where my twentieth-anniversary band used to be. Six months earlier, that ring had held so much promise.

I'd met my husband when I was sixteen. James was eighteen and had just moved to our small town in Florida. His parents had been missionaries. He grew up in Africa. I'd dream myself into his stories of helping people in a faraway land.

We fell in love and got engaged. It was the biggest thing that had ever happened to me. I was twenty. I felt like the curtain had finally gone up on my life. Then, after a routine checkup, I was diagnosed with Type 1 diabetes. I faced a lifetime of taking insulin shots and managing my disease. *Thank God I have James* was all I could think.

We began our marriage with a U-Haul full of wedding presents as our only possessions. I worked in banking. James was in sales. James's dream of going back to Africa faded into the background. After our son and daughter were born, we settled down in Georgia, and James started a manufacturer's rep business out of our home. I loved that he was there when I came home from my administrative job at our church. As for my diabetes, I had flare-ups, but my health was pretty stable. Most of our friends were from our church, including the first couple we got to know in the area. The woman became James's secretary. James and I taught Sunday school and Bible-study classes together. Like everything, it was always easier with him beside me.

Before I knew it, I'd spent more years of my life with James than without him. The night before my thirty-ninth birthday I lay in bed thinking, *One more year and I'll be forty.* I was proud of my life, content as a wife and mother. Yet forty had hit James hard. His mother had just died and middle age left him feeling restless and withdrawn. I even wondered if he was depressed. But James had always been there for me. Now I would be there for him. I turned on my side and peered at him in the dark. "James, do you want to talk? What's bothering you?"

He sighed. "Well...I guess you have a right to know."

He told me he was having an affair with our friend, the secretary. All at once I felt like I was outside myself watching two people in bed talking. James stared rigidly up at the ceiling as he related the details. My heart pounded. A cauldron of emotions churned within me—rage, hurt, jealousy, disbelief. But one dominated them all—fear. Fear that James would leave me. A terrible frantic fear that I would be alone.

"I'm not sure how I feel right now—about anything," he said finally.

I turned to him in the darkness. Of all the things I wanted to say, only one came out: "Please don't leave us."

I stumbled out of bed, went into the bathroom, and threw up. Was I having an insulin reaction? Shakily I tested my blood sugar. Normal. I crept downstairs and lay on the sofa, staring into the cold, dark fireplace. I didn't sleep. I hardly moved. Morning came at last, pale and damp.

Terrified, I watched James leave to talk to the other woman. It turned out that she didn't want to leave her husband and broke off the affair. But James said he still needed time to think. He emptied out his side of the closet and carried his suitcases down to the car, our fifteen-year-old daughter's sunken red eyes following him, our ten-year-old son too young to understand why Daddy was leaving.

He'll come around, I kept telling myself. But in the mornings I'd wake up to the empty space beside me and panic would rise in me like a scream. *Lord, please let him come back.*

Three weeks later, James called. He wanted to come home. *Thank You, Lord, for this miracle.* I quit my job so I could be his new secretary. I got books about communication, trust, and couples who'd survived infidelity. James and I were going to be one of those couples.

The other woman and her husband left the area, and we moved into a new home, one without memories. Still, each time

James took me in his arms, a battle raged inside of me. I wanted to believe each touch was a promise that he'd never leave me again, that God had been merciful. As soon as he let go of me, fear took hold. I was afraid to relax even long after he breathed in the slow, steady rhythm of sleep, afraid I'd wake up in the morning to find him gone, a note on the pillow, his side of the closet emptied out again.

On our twentieth anniversary, James gave me a beautiful ring—one large, brilliant diamond surrounded by eight tiny ones. "Oh, James," I whispered, slipping off my wedding ring and putting the anniversary ring on in its place. Surely this was the reassurance I'd been praying for, a sign from God that James was committed to our marriage. I felt confident again. I learned to play golf, went on business trips with him, and decorated the new house.

One fall Sunday we pulled into our garage after church. The kids rushed inside. "I need to talk to you," James said. The tone of his voice made my stomach churn just as it had that night eighteen months earlier. "I've tried," he said bluntly, "but I can't do it. I want a divorce."

Part of me wanted to slap his face. Yet I stood frozen in place, paralyzed by fear. Still, I couldn't bring myself to beg this time.

Once again the kids and I watched James pack his things and drive away. I went to my room and lay down in the center of the bed. I looked at my anniversary ring. A fake. Worthless. That's what it was. I took it off and dumped it in a drawer.

I pushed on, taking care of the children and landing a new job. But every time I paused to think—to make a decision about the kids or even just pay the mortgage—panic hit me. *You're alone now.*

Within a month my health collapsed. My blood sugar destabilized, and I found myself lying in that cold hospital bed— listening to the monotonous sound of the heart monitor, the dull, relentless mechanics of my heart.

I closed my eyes. I listened to the beeps. What an incredible thing, I suddenly thought. A calmness and peace came over me. My heartbeat. Such an easy thing to take for granted. Each beat, though, each little beep was a gift, wasn't it? Broken or not, my heart continued, life continued. I breathed in and out, deeply. God was responsible for every beat of my heart. I felt Him nearer to me now than ever, nearer than anyone. He was there, as close as the air I breathed.

That was the miracle of God's love. God would never leave me. His love is constant. I was no longer afraid. Instead of abandoned I felt embraced, empowered now by God's love to start life anew. Each beat of my heart was another step.

Several years later, my life is full. Full not with a false sense of security but with the strength of a greater love. On my left ring finger I wear a ring. It is the same anniversary ring my ex-husband gave me. I had the center stone replaced with a heart-shaped amethyst birthstone. Like me, it is remade—and a reminder of a love that will never end.

Precious and Permanent

*We are so preciously loved by
God that we cannot even comprehend it.
No created being can ever know how much
and how sweetly and tenderly
God loves them.*

JULIAN OF NORWICH

Somebody Needs You

BY E. STANLEY JONES

I believe the most dramatic moment in history occurred two thousand years ago, as a little group of listeners leaned forward to hear Jesus' answer to a certain question. There were 3,600 commandments at that time in the Jewish law; the question they had put to Jesus was, "Which one is the greatest?"

It was not only a matter of great import to the Jews of those days; on His answer would depend the place He would hold in our lives today. Would it be the answer of a man speaking to his moment in history, or would it be God's answer, true for all time? The Bible, of course, records Jesus' reply. Jesus said:

"Thou shalt love...."

What kind of an answer is it, in the world we live in? In the 1960s, a leading American psychiatrist, Karl Menninger, took a walk through his sanitarium in Kansas. Here were men and women whose problems had driven them to this retreat from the world. As he walked through the buildings and the grounds, Dr. Menninger asked himself, "Why are they here?" The theory had been that they didn't understand themselves, therefore insight was the answer. But now Menninger had a new idea: what if they were there because they'd never loved or been loved? What if that were the disease?

On this suspicion, he organized the whole sanitarium on a new basis. He told the staff, "We've been giving these people understanding when perhaps what they need is love. From the chief psychiatrist down to the gardener, all our contacts for a while are going to be love contacts. If you go into a patient's room to change a light bulb, go in with an attitude of love."

After six months they took stock to see how the new system was working: they discovered that the average period of hospitalization had been cut in half.

Some years later, a newspaper reporter in Tucson, Arizona, asked Dr. Menninger this question, "Suppose you suspect that you're heading for a nervous breakdown. What should you do?"

You'd have thought that a great psychiatrist would have said, "Go see a psychiatrist." But this is what he did say: "Go straight to your front door, turn the knob, go outside, and find somebody who needs you."

In other words, the finding of psychiatry was that the mind breaks down when love breaks down. Medical doctors were beginning to discover that the body can break down for the same reason. A New York businessman I've known for many years went to his doctor for pains in his neck and shoulders. After examining him the doctor wrote out this prescription: "Go down to Grand Central Station, find someone in trouble, and do something for him."

The businessman snorted. But he'd paid money for that advice so he thought he'd better follow it. He went down to

Grand Central and there in a corner was a woman sitting on a suitcase and weeping. He went up to her and said, "Madam, may I do something for you?"

At first she was too embarrassed to answer. He was embarrassed too, but he kept at it and finally learned that this was her first trip to New York, her daughter was not there to meet her, and the size of the station had confused and frightened her. He got the daughter's name, went to a telephone book and looked up the address, helped the lady into a cab, bought her some flowers on the way, and delivered her to the daughter who had lost her mother's letter and had spent two days waiting in Pennsylvania Station.

My friend went back to his doctor and said, "Say, Doc, that was awfully good medicine. My neck feels better already."

Psychiatry and medicine were revealing a picture of man that was not different from the one Jesus drew. In fact, the more science taught us about ourselves, the more we saw His commandment in a new light: not as a difficult assignment for those advanced in the religious life but as a very condition of life itself.

If this is so, then failure to love should be as fatal as failure to breathe. And this is just what doctors in New York's Bellevue Hospital found some years ago. The staff on the children's ward made the tragic discovery that they were losing 32 percent of the children under a year old, mostly through minor ailments. The doctors were dumbfounded. They were giving the infants scientific treatment, scientific feeding, sterile surroundings, and they were dying.

At last someone suggested that what the hospital environment was not supplying was love. So they sent out a call for "love-volunteers": women to come and love babies for so many hours a day. Hundreds of women responded because they had a need too: the need for someone to love. In most instances they were older women whose own children had grown up and who had no one now to love but themselves or some distant grandchildren. So they volunteered and the death-rate began to plunge. After four months the superintendent said, "We could no more do without these love-volunteers than we could do without penicillin."

Now the interesting thing is that love always works as it did with these children in Bellevue Hospital: it is always specific. It is always one woman rocking one particular baby; no one has yet learned how to love people in general. I described the Bellevue experiment in a lecture in Sweden one day and a nurse in the audience came to me afterwards and told me this story.

When she first went to work in a government convalescent home years earlier, she'd been assigned to an elderly patient who had not spoken a single word in three years. The other nurses disliked this patient so much that she was always passed down to the newest member of the staff. But this nurse was a Christian, or at least she'd always thought she was, and she decided that her Christian love was only as good as her love for this particular patient.

The old woman used to sit in a rocking chair all day long. "So I pulled up another rocking chair," the nurse said, "and just rocked alongside her and loved her and loved her and loved her." The third day she opened her eyes and said, "You're so kind."

Those were the first words she had spoken in three years. In two weeks she was out of the home. Now I never saw the patient whose life was transformed by love, but I did see the nurse who did the loving, and here is another of the unarguable truths about love: it makes the lover beautiful.

The great Christian writer and speaker Rufus Moseley used to say, "You are born of the qualities you habitually give out. If you give out hate, you become hateful. If you give out criticism, you become critical. If you give out love, you become lovely. So give out love and only love."

Somebody asked him once, "But Mr. Moseley, suppose they won't take your love?"

His answer: "Increase the dose."

It sounds too simple, put like that. And here is both the glory and the peril of Christ's commandment to love. The glory of it is that we may finally learn enough simplicity to follow it. The peril is that we will try to expand on it. Jesus reduced 3,600 commandments to one; right away the temptation of Christian writers and thinkers was to start putting the others back.

They were tempted, but they didn't give in—not the great ones. It looked for a while as though Paul was making faith as important as love in the new church. But there came a moment when Paul had to select the supreme value and he took the torch from his Master and wrote, "Now abide faith, hope, love, these three; but the greatest of these is love" (1 Corinthians 13:13 NASB).

There was another perilous moment when John began to write, because it looked as though the most important thing in his theology was going to be knowledge. He was writing for a generation of Gnostics, people who believed you didn't have to have an Incarnation—you could arrive at all truth within yourself. The Gnostics were the Knowers.

John wrote a great deal about knowledge, but he wrote something else, something that had never been written before, and I think all heaven leaned over the battlements to see whether he would write it. And when he did I think heaven broke out cheering, "Oh, they've got it! At last they've got it!" For John had written:

"God is love."

John was in the little group that held their breath to hear the great commandment. And I like to think that afterward he puzzled over it, as we all do when we hear it for the first time.

Is this what God requires of us? Is this the highest thing on earth?

I like to think that later, when Jesus' earthly life was over, John woke up in the middle of one cold, starry night and said, "Of course. We are made in the image of God; if we could only see Him we would know what we must be. I have seen Him. I know."

The Greatest Love

*"Teacher, which is the greatest
commandment in the Law?"
Jesus replied: "'Love the Lord your
God with all your heart and with all your
soul and with all your mind.' This is the
first and greatest commandment.
And the second is like it:
'Love your neighbor as yourself.'"*

MATTHEW 22:36–39 NIV

Six Days

BY SUZANNE SHEMWELL

*C*an't live with him, can't live without him. That was the story of my life with Jim. Twenty-three years we'd been together—twenty-three years of adventure and aggravation, big blowups and equally passionate making up. We got divorced only to fall in love with each other again and remarry. I'd thought it would be different this second time around, that I could count on Jim to be my partner with our three kids, the house, the finances, our faith. But he let me take care of everything, like always. Happy-go-lucky Jim. Well, I didn't feel so happy or lucky. *Lord, I can't live like this anymore*, I prayed. *Is it finally over between us? Is that what You're trying to tell me?*

Still, I'd agreed to take this Wednesday off and go snowmobiling with him. Maybe it was just for old times' sake. He said we'd get an early start so we could get in plenty of time outdoors before we had to pick up our youngest, eight-year-old Taryn, from day care. He just had to run a few errands first. It was almost noon already.

Finally his truck pulled up. I tried to control my irritation. "You still want to go? We have to get Taryn by six thirty."

"Come on, Suz," Jim cajoled. "We'll just go up to Pilot Peak for two or three hours. It'll be fun."

Fun. That's all he thinks about, I grumbled silently, but I helped him load gear into the truck. About forty miles outside Boise we picked up some snacks—cheese sticks, candy bars, cocktail sausages, water, and Gatorade. We parked four miles from Pilot Peak. It was snowing but not enough to worry about. We unloaded the snowmobiles and hit the trail. As usual, I took the lead. I came up to a ridge overlooking an untouched valley. I throttled my engine down and waited for Jim to catch up.

"Want to explore?" I asked. Jim nodded. The two of us went off the groomed trail. It was a rush, zooming down the steep hill, the wind and snow blasting in our faces. Then we got stuck. The snow was coming down pretty heavily. "Let's go back up," I said. We dug our sleds out and headed uphill. Neither of us could get enough traction to make it to the top.

"Maybe we should head down first. We can follow that creek," Jim said, pointing downhill, "find a trail and wind our way back up to Pilot Peak."

Jim went first. I followed his tracks. I came around a turn and saw him standing in the creek. He waved, shaking his head sheepishly. He was okay but the slope was so steep, he'd slid into the water.

"We need to pile up snow under my sled so we can get it out of the creek," Jim said. It took two hours to work the machine out of the water and get moving again. *Crash!* I ran into a tree and bounced off the sled. I sat in the snow and caught my breath. I looked at my watch. "Jim, it's after four. We're not going to get out of here in time to pick up Taryn."

"Don't worry, the day care will call Dorinda. She'll take care of her little sister," Jim said. His expression grew serious. "Suz, we're not going to make it home tonight. We've got to get out of the elements."

Great, I thought. *Another one of his messes.* But I wasn't about to start a fight.

Jim went to look for firewood. I made a snow cave big enough for the two of us. Jim came back with an armful of branches and twigs. He built a big fire in front of the cave and a smaller fire inside. We tried to dry off. Jim dozed off. *Typical*, I thought, poking at the fire. *He leaves all the work to me. How could I have married him once, let alone twice!* If the fire went out, we'd freeze to death. I didn't sleep a wink.

Morning came. We dug my machine out. I said to Jim, "We need to pray." We grabbed hands and asked God to give us the strength and wisdom to get out of there, and to comfort our daughters. We took off. Suddenly, Jim rammed into a tree. He landed on his back and clutched his knee. "Jim!" I cried out.

"I'm all right, Honey," he said, wincing.

We continued on. Then my machine got stuck. We had to abandon it and ride on his. We fought our way through the snow until dark. We'd have to stop for the night. Jim collected firewood and I dug a snow cave. Just like last night, except this time I slept a little. The next morning we finished the last of our food. We couldn't get Jim's machine moving again in the sticky snow.

"Let's just bag the snowmobile and walk out the way we came," I said. We gathered everything we thought we could use—lighters, my whistle, the shovel, shop rags, the tow rope. "Wait," Jim said. He siphoned gas into one of our empty water bottles and soaked the shop rags in oil. We could use these as fire starters. *Good thinking*, I admitted.

It was easier to walk in the snowmobile tracks. Pretty soon we came to the snow cave we'd slept in the night before.

"I can't believe it took us fifteen minutes to double back. We spent five hours struggling to travel that far!" I could hear the discouragement in my own voice.

"We're going to get off this mountain, Suz," Jim said. "Let's stay here tonight and get some rest."

We repaired the snow cave. "Sleep," Jim said. "I'll watch the fire first." I was too tired to argue. Too tired to even pray, though I knew that God was our only hope. *Was Jim praying? Was he as scared as I was?* I leaned against him and drifted off.

We took turns napping and tending the fire. Outside, the snow was coming down hard. During my shift I watched Jim sleep. Even in the flickering firelight I could see the exhaustion etched into his face. *He's given his all to keep us alive*, I marveled. There we were, in the worst predicament of our lives, yet we hadn't had a single fight. For once we were truly working together.

The next morning, I told Jim, "Honey, we're not going to get out of here without God's help."

Jim took my hands and bowed his head. "Lord, we really need You. I got us into this mess and You're going to have to get us out. Help us get home to our girls. I need to get Suzanne home safely." His sweet prayer brought tears to my eyes.

Jim trudged ahead of me, blocking the wind and tramping down the snow so it was easier for me to follow. We took a break. Remembering Jim's prayer, I asked, "Do you feel responsible for me?"

"Yes," Jim said. "If only I hadn't made us turn down that hill..."

"No," I said, "you're the reason I'm still standing." Jim hugged me close, and for a moment I didn't feel the cold at all.

That evening we stopped to make camp. A plane! We waved our helmets and shovel in the air like mad. I blew my whistle. Twenty minutes later we heard a helicopter. They must have seen us. We were going home! But the chopper flew past. I heard it disappear in the distance, taking our hopes with it.

"Are we going to make it back to our girls?" I asked Jim.

"We will make it home," Jim answered, his voice never wavering. "Trust me. The Lord won't leave us out here."

Sunday morning we hit another steep slope. No way up except to crawl. I followed Jim, clawing snow until my arms ached. "Jim, I can't go any farther."

"Suz, you can," he said. He grabbed my gear and put it in his pack. He looped the snowmobile tow rope around his shoulder and tied the other end to my wrist. "We're in this together, Suz." Each step he took, Jim pulled his weight and then some. He got us to the top of that hill. That night Jim nestled me in a snow cave and tended the fire all by himself. *Dear Lord, thank You for Jim.*

Monday morning Jim announced, "I guess I'll have my coffee now." What was he talking about? He knew as well as I did we were out of food and water. He scooped up a handful of snow and popped it into his mouth.

I laughed. I couldn't help it. "Yeah, me too," I said. "I think I want some bacon and eggs with mine." Never had I felt more grateful that I'd married a man who had a sense of humor.

That afternoon, Jim saw Pilot Peak in the distance. "We're almost there, hon," he told me. "We're going to make it."

Then Jim stopped and said, "Listen, do you hear that?" Snowmobiles!

Jim took off running. I started hollering and blowing my whistle.

Soon two guys from a search party came roaring up. They pulled out oranges, granola bars, jerky, and water. Jim gave me the water and tugged off his gloves. He peeled an orange and tenderly placed the fruit in my hand.

"I love you, Suz," Jim said. "We're going to make it, you know."

"I love you too," I said.

I know my husband wasn't just talking about our ordeal in the wilderness. It will take even more working and praying together than those six days in the snow, but we are rebuilding our marriage. After all, this is the man I married twice.

Building Love

Love requires sharing,
Sharing requires struggle,
Struggle requires faith,
Faith requires love.

Kiss of Faith

BY GENELL DAWSON

L ate on that Sunday afternoon in October 2000 the phone rang. My husband, Clyde, had promised to be home ages ago. *What now?* I thought.

"Maybe Dad stopped to buy you a birthday present," my daughter, Amber, offered, picking up the receiver. I rolled my eyes. My birthday was still five days away, and Amber knew just as well as I did that Clyde always put off buying gifts until the last minute. I checked my watch. Already four thirty. Typical workaholic Clyde. If he wasn't logging overtime as a facilities engineer at the local Toyota plant like today, he was working through our church, even spending his last few vacations on mission trips in Mexico and Russia.

Amber turned to me, a strange look on her face, and held out the phone. "It's Mission Hospital," she said. "They want to talk to you—about Dad."

Clyde had been in a car accident. I was praying for him before I even hung up the phone. Amber and I jumped in the car. I rattled off numbers as I drove. Rev. Dudley Bristow from our old church; my boss and good friend, Janet; people from our current congregation. Amber called them on the cell.

Lately it seemed Clyde and I spent what little time we did have together arguing about the time we spent apart. We always kissed and made up in the end, though. After almost twenty years, that simple act was still a powerful reminder of the love that had drawn us together. *Please, God,* I prayed, pulling up to the hospital, *give us more time.*

The chaplain came to talk to us. "Your husband has been critically injured and is in surgery," she said. "You need to get his family here as soon as you can."

We made more frantic calls. Our older daughter, Michelle, at college in Arizona. Clyde's twin brother, Curt, and their older brother, Jerry. Our family physician, Dr. Pino. One thought kept going through my mind: was Clyde still alive? In the background the same prayer repeated steadily like a heartbeat: *please, God, give us more time.*

By 1:00 a.m. more than one hundred family and friends were gathered in the waiting area. Finally a surgeon with blood on his scrubs, his deeply lined eyes just visible over his mask, emerged from the operating suite and took me aside. "Mrs. Dawson, your husband has suffered grave injuries. He's been lacerated from his ribs to his pelvic bone back to his spine. His stomach, liver, and kidneys are badly damaged. We've done everything we can, but he's in a coma. I'm very sorry, but I don't think he will make it through the night."

All that got through to me at that moment was that Clyde was still alive. And that meant he could be healed. "I have my faith," I said.

The doctor sighed. "You're going to need more than that, I'm afraid," he said.

I'd relied on my faith my entire life, taking strength in knowing that God could help me through anything. Now my husband was dying and his doctor was telling me not even God could save his life. *What if it really was too late? What if there was nothing more even God could do?* The prayer circling my mind continued, longer now. *Please, God, give us more time. Give me whatever I need to help Clyde.*

They let me see Clyde. It was hard to tell where the tubes and machines ended and he began. A tube was down his throat so I couldn't kiss him, and I had to wear protective gloves just to touch him. When I reached to stroke his brow, the nurse stopped me. "Be careful. His bones are fractured," she said.

I drew back and choked out, "I'm sorry," then fled to the waiting room.

I couldn't sleep, even with a sedative. Thank goodness my sister-in-law had brought my Bible and prayer journal.

The nurses allowed me five minutes of visiting time each hour and, at first, that was all I could bear. During the day Amber or Michelle or a friend from church would go into the ICU with me. At night it was just Clyde and me. The more I sat with my husband the harder it was to leave when the nurses asked.

On the third night, I pulled off the gloves, hoping Clyde would respond to my touch. I stroked his cheek, his forehead, the scraggly hair growing out of his chin. "Keep holding on, baby.

Only twenty more days till our twentieth anniversary." I even wrote that in my journal.

The fifth day I remarked to a nurse as I sat with Clyde, "The doctor didn't think he'd make it through the first night. Maybe he'll wake up soon."

The nurse reached out and touched my shoulder. "Mrs. Dawson, I think it's important you understand your husband is still in very critical condition," she said. "He's on dialysis, his spleen has been removed, and his other organs are shutting down one by one. I'm sorry, but he's far from waking up."

Back in the waiting room friends and family surprised me with a cake. My birthday. How could I celebrate my birth when my husband was dying? I excused myself to talk to Dr. Pino. "Please, you've got to be honest with me," I begged him.

He shook his head slowly. "Genell, you need to prepare for the worst."

I felt my knees buckle. Only through the most intense prayer had I been able to keep it together these past five days. But things were getting worse, not better. Clyde was still holding on. How would I? *God, I don't know how to pray any harder. Give me more faith.*

The nurses stopped asking me to leave after five minutes. I bathed and shaved Clyde as best I could around the tubes and bandages. "You're wasting away. Wouldn't you like to wake up and have a chile relleno right now?" I asked. One day I picked up his hand and pressed it to my lips. "You already missed my birthday. You don't want to miss our anniversary too, do you?" I felt so connected to him that it seemed like his body was an extension of my own, that it was my breath flowing into him.

It was the same way with my prayers. I prayed so deeply that prayer became less of an act than a state of being. And I was surrounded by hundreds of others praying for my husband's recovery—relatives, friends, our church family, even people in Mexico and Russia whom Clyde had met on his mission trips. We prayed for Clyde's organs one by one. "Help Clyde's kidneys work again, Lord. Heal the damage to his liver." We prayed for his foot, and the doctors saved it even though it was broken in dozens of places and had become gangrenous.

Another five days passed, but now I knew better than to think that meant Clyde was out of the woods. Instead I took joy in the little things. Like being able to kiss him again. A tracheotomy allowed the tube to come out of his throat at last. His facial muscles were still tensed up in a grimace so I massaged around his mouth, hoping to ease it into a smile. "I love you, Clyde. I'm sorry about all the times we ever argued," I said. "Please wake up, baby." I rested my head on the pillow beside his. And I felt not Clyde but God answer me. *Be still and trust Me.*

On day twenty-one I went home to shower, but then it was right back to the ICU, to Clyde. I nodded to the nurse and turned to look at my husband. I'd just given him a bath and shave, and he looked rested. I bent down to kiss him hello like always. Just before I pulled away, I thought I felt his lips move. I drew back and stared at him. His eyes were still closed. Again I kissed him. He puckered up and kissed me back! Clyde had kissed me back! And that kiss was a promise, just like the kiss that sealed our wedding vows twenty years earlier. Except this time the promise was not so much from Clyde as from God, that He was returning my husband to me, that He was giving us more time after all.

"Nurse, my husband kissed me!"

"It's likely just a reflex," she said.

"No, watch," I insisted. I kissed Clyde and again he puckered his lips and kissed me back.

The nurse's eyes widened. "I have to get the doctor."

I kissed Clyde twice more before the doctor came. Then I kissed him again. He kissed me back. The doctor squeezed Clyde's hand. He squeezed back. Later that same day Clyde started to wake up. Two days later, on October 31, we marked our twentieth anniversary. "We'll spend the next twenty years together, won't we, baby?" I asked. Clyde still couldn't talk, but for me his kiss was answer enough.

I'd sat by my husband's bedside those long days not knowing if he would wake up again. The doctor had been right. My faith had not been enough. But all I had to do was reach out and ask, and I received more than I ever could have imagined. God gives us faith as generously as He gives His love. And both know no bounds.

Boundless Love

*The resource from which [God] gives is
boundless, measureless,
unlimited, unending,
abundant, almighty,
and eternal.*

JACK HAYFORD

Marion's Marriage

BY MARION BOND WEST

As I approached my fourth year of being a widow, my son Jon said to me one day, "Mom, you should attend singles meetings. Go somewhere. How will you ever meet anyone?"

I sat at the old oak kitchen table with Jon as he devoured a sandwich. "I can't, Jon. I just can't take a casserole and go to a singles meeting. I didn't like boy/girl parties when I was thirteen. I still don't like them. God's going to have to send someone to me."

"That's crazy, Mom. Do you really think you can just sit here day after day and someone will knock on your door and say, 'Hello. I'm your Christian husband-to-be, sent by God'?"

I brightened. Sounded good to me. "Yes, Jon! That's exactly what I'll do."

"Aw, Mom, be reasonable. You have to date."

I'd dated some. I didn't even like the word for someone my age who'd been married for twenty-five years. Jon left for work and I sat alone, thinking. *Lord,* I said, *I do not want to date. I just want to be a wife again. And I don't want to get married simply for companionship. I want a real romance. You select him. You know me better than I know myself.*

About the middle of last March I added a list of some qualifications for the husband I wanted:

1. God must be first in his life. I want to be second.
2. He's well-read and loves books.
3. Further along than I am spiritually.
4. I'd like to be a minister's wife, but I'll leave that up to You.
5. He has a deep sense of humor so that we can laugh a lot.
6. He's able to communicate and have long conversations.
7. Cares about people, especially people who are hurting.
8. He will allow me to write and speak as long as You want me to.
9. He needs me.
10. There must be romance. Sparks!

In the weeks that followed, thoughts that I believed were from God eased into my mind. *I'm going to answer your prayer for a husband.... The answer will come very quickly—so fast it will scare you if you don't trust Me completely.... The answer will come through a phone call from a Guideposts reader in response to an article.*

When will I know for certain, Lord? I asked.

By your birthday.

So by July 8 I should know something.

In April *Guideposts* published my article on depression. That article evoked responses from quite a few men going through the pain of losing their wives. Phone calls and letters became fairly common—from the Atlanta, Georgia, area, as well as other states.

On April 8 I received a telephone call from a professor of sociology at Oklahoma State University in Stillwater. He lived on a small farm with some cattle, a grown son and a red dog. He was also a minister. Our conversations quickly became a regular thing, three or four times a week. I was corresponding with several other men too as a result of the article and had gone out with several from the Atlanta area But pretty soon the professor/minister/ farmer and I were writing almost every day. Our letters weren't love letters exactly, but there always seemed to be something between the lines, and I easily understood the unwritten messages.

Sometimes Gene Acuff enclosed a blank sheet of paper without explanation. "What's the blank paper?" I finally wrote.

His answer was immediate: "Things I want to say to you that you aren't yet ready to hear."

Gene planned to come to Atlanta to see me. He says that I invited him, but I didn't. "What do you want to see?" I asked. "Where do you want to go?"

"I just want to see you. No parties, no big plans. I want to walk with you, talk and laugh. I want to sit in a porch swing with you, and I'd like to go somewhere under a tin roof and listen to the rain with you." I was smiling as I held the phone. I smiled a lot when we talked. We were talking six to eight hours weekly. My mother said I had a certain light back in my eyes again.

Of course, I carefully told myself this wasn't serious. We didn't really know each other. We'd just get acquainted, have some good conversation and good food, and relate our experiences of grief and loss. Gene's wife of twenty-five years had died in February of an eleven-day brain-related illness. His loss was much too recent for us to be serious. I had no way of knowing then that when Gene read my article on depression in the April *Guideposts*, God spoke to him: *Check your wife's Bible. If she has the same Scriptures underlined that Marion used in the article, phone her right away.* She did, and he did. Although neither of us understands it or can explain it, he says God told him then, *She will be your new wife.*

On my fifty-first birthday I went to get the mail as soon as I saw the mailman put it in the box. I knew a letter from Gene would arrive. He'd already sent me a dozen red roses. There had been some mention of photographs. So far, all I had was a very small family portrait taken several years ago. I wanted some new pictures but wouldn't ask for them.

There were two letters, one so thick I knew it was the promised pictures. I was late for an appointment and it was terribly hot, so I sat in my car with the air conditioning going full blast and read the letters. Just as I opened the pictures, God seemed to say, *Put the tape lying on the seat in the tape deck.* I glanced on the seat. Yes, there lay a tape. Several days earlier all my Christian tapes had been stolen. The police returned them a few days later and by mistake included a country-and-western tape, which I'd meant to give back. I'm definitely not a country-and-western music fan. But I knew Gene was, and I had this funny feeling that something big was about to happen. Playing this tape seemed absolutely crazy, but this whole adventure with Gene Acuff was crazy, so I put the tape in.

Jim Reeves began to sing incredibly sweet songs about love, including an old favorite I hadn't even thought about since I was sixteen: "Evening shadows make me blue, when each weary day is through...how I long to be with you...my happiness."

Tears blurred my vision, and I whispered aloud over my pounding heart, "God, You can't possibly be speaking to me through a stolen country-and-western tape!" I had the photographs in my hand. I looked intently at Gene's smiling face and then at his dog. The dog was smiling too! His expression clearly said, *He's pretty wonderful.* Gene wrote, "If I could take you out on your birthday, I'd pick you up in my old '41 Chevy and we'd go to a 1950s movie and eat popcorn and drink Cokes from the little bottles, and of course we'd eat Milk Duds at the movies."

"Milk Duds," I screamed over the music, my heart melting like hot butter. No one knew of my passion for Milk Duds. How could Gene Acuff know? Jim Reeves was singing "Have I Told You Lately That I Love You?" I was humming along and trying not to cry on the photograph—as I drove to my appointment an hour late.

That night Gene phoned, and as we were about to hang up he said for the first time, "I love you, Marion." "Thank you, 'bye," I answered curtly and hung up. He said the same thing two nights later, and I said the same thing. Only this time I hid under my pillow after hanging up and said, "Oh, God, I don't know how to handle this." The third time he told me he loved me, there was a long silence. Then Gene asked, "Are you going to say what I want you to say?" I took a deep breath. I knew I loved him. It was as though I were a child about to jump off a high dive that I'd tried to jump from many times during the summer. "I love you, Professor Acuff. I really do love you." I had often wondered what his response would be if I ever said those words. His response wasn't to me at all: "Thank You, Lord. Oh, thank You. Praise You, Lord Jesus."

July 27, the date of Gene's planned arrival, finally came. The waiting had been almost unbearable. I had lost twelve pounds and was hardly sleeping. The phone rang at noon, right on schedule, and a voice I knew so well said, "Hello."

"Where are you?" I asked.

"Stone Mountain Inn."

"I'll be there in ten minutes." Driving to the inn, I could hardly believe it was finally happening. We were actually going to meet. Stone Mountain Inn is a resort just ten minutes from my house. I pulled in the driveway. Someone honked at me. Looking in the rearview mirror, I recognized Gene. I thought about sitting in the car and letting him come over. But just like in the movies, we moved very fast toward each other. I left my car running in the middle of a driveway, the door open. My sunglasses dropped on the pavement. Just as we embraced, I remembered some strict advice I'd given my girls when they were growing up: "No public display of affection, ever." But right then in the middle of the parking lot in broad daylight with people all around us, we kissed. I lost count of the times.

I had planned a picnic for just the two of us the next day at my cousin's 150-year-old renovated farmhouse located on 600 acres in northeast Georgia. It is a getaway for them, furnished in antiques. I thought Gene would feel at home there. There were even cattle and three swings and a tin roof. Sitting on a quaint love seat in front of a stone fireplace, Gene started to ask if I would marry him in December.

I suddenly experienced a full-fledged ulcer attack. The stress had been unbearable. We were deeply in love and knew God had brought us together. But he had to return to Oklahoma to teach, and I didn't see how I could just pull up stakes and go with him. My two boys, almost twenty, lived with me. I was paranoid about leaving them alone for even a night, certain they would break some of my rules. Also, my two married daughters and two granddaughters lived nearby. Jennifer, the younger daughter, was expecting her first child. My widowed mother lived less than an hour and a half away. All my dearest friends, my world, was in Georgia. I'd always lived there. And I was booked to speak for the next six months.

Gene had to move to the far end of the love seat. Every time he came close my stomach pains intensified. He held onto my foot and asked me to marry him. I found I could tolerate foot-holding pretty well. I said yes. We talked about maintaining two separate residences and commuting often. Two days later, in exactly two minutes, we selected an engagement ring.

Then it was Sunday. Our week was over. Gene left, crying. I went to my room, crying, and fell across my bed begging

God to "do something." He somehow knocked me out. Totally. Meanwhile Gene, en route to Oklahoma, phoned, but my boys couldn't wake me up. When I did wake up four hours later and they told me he'd called, I somehow knew I must clear my calendar. I started phoning people, asking to be relieved of speaking engagements. In eleven years of speaking, I'd never done such a thing except when my husband, Jerry, had brain surgery.

Later Gene called again from Tennessee and asked, "Could you marry me Wednesday of next week?" I checked my calendar and wrote "Marry Gene" on August 12.

As it turned out, the date was moved to August 14 at seven in the evening. A small ceremony was planned. Gene never asked me to leave my boys. He was content to have a marriage in which we commuted for a while. But God told me clearly, *Quit hovering over your boys. You are trying to be their god. Let Me be God to them.*

Gene and I honeymooned at my cousin's old restored farmhouse. I guess you could say we identified with it. The farmhouse never expected to be restored and alive again with meaning and purpose. Gene and I understood something about restoration. We thought the farmhouse might like us too. Together we were almost 107 years old. The night before we left the farm, God sent the rain we'd so often talked about on the phone and written about. It was our first time to see rain together. As we listened to it on the tin roof, Gene said quietly, "Your formula works, Marion."

"What formula?"

"The restoration formula from your book, *The Nevertheless Principle*."

Oh, yes! Yes, it did work. I could remember the formula almost word for word. When I was slowly watching my husband die from a brain tumor, I carefully examined my restoration formula:

> No matter what is taken away from you, if you keep your eyes on Jesus and praise Him, He will restore it to you. You will be joyful to the exact same degree you have hurt. What you have lost will be replaced: joy for mourning...beauty for ashes....
>
> *God, I don't see how it could possibly work now. I don't see how You will ever come to me again in any shape or form. But I won't limit You, so I'm going to remember this moment for the rest of my life. And if and when You restore the years that the locusts have eaten, I will tell people about it and write about it. I am committing to You to remember this agony, and if You can come up with some kind of joy to the equivalent that I hurt, You are truly a God of miracles.*

On August 22, 1987, Gene and I headed for the Atlanta airport and a new life together. I'd often said after Jerry was gone that if God ever asked me to simply walk out on everything, I would. But I had assumed that it would be for missions—Africa, not Stillwater, Oklahoma! But God had recently given me an old familiar Scripture with a marvelous life-changing message: "The Lord is my shepherd; I shall not want.... He leadeth me beside the 'Stillwaters.' He restoreth my soul."

My Heart's Love

My heart is like a singing bird
Whose nest is in a watered shoot;
My heart is like an apple tree
Whose boughs are bent with thickset fruit;
My heart is like a rainbow shell
That paddles in a halcyon sea;
My heart is gladder than all these
Because my love is come to me.

CHRISTINA ROSSETTI

A Note from the Editors

Guideposts, a nonprofit organization, touches millions of lives every day through products and services that inspire, encourage, and uplift. Our magazines, books, prayer network, and outreach programs help people connect their faith-filled values to their daily lives. To learn more, visit Guideposts.org or GuidepostsFoundation.org.